1881447339 11/6/07

D0457010

OUT OF RANGE

Out of Range

. . .

WHY THE CONSTITUTION

CAN'T END THE BATTLE OVER GUNS

Mark V. Tushnet

OXFORD
UNIVERSITY PRESS

2007

OXFORD

UNIVERSITY PRESS

Oxford University Press, Inc., publishes works that further
Oxford University's objective of excellence
in research, scholarship, and education.

Oxford   New York
Auckland   Cape Town   Dar es Salaam   Hong Kong   Karachi
Kuala Lumpur   Madrid   Melbourne   Mexico City   Nairobi
New Delhi   Shanghai   Taipei   Toronto

With offices in
Argentina   Austria   Brazil   Chile   Czech Republic   France   Greece
Guatemala   Hungary   Italy   Japan   Poland   Portugal   Singapore
South Korea   Switzerland   Thailand   Turkey   Ukraine   Vietnam

Copyright (c) 2007 by Oxford University Press, Inc.
Published by Oxford University Press, Inc.
198 Madison Avenue, New York, New York 10016
www.oup.com

Library of Congress Cataloging-in-Publication Data
Tushnet, Mark V., 1945–
Out of range : why the Constitution can't end the battle
over guns / Mark V. Tushnet.
p.   cm.—(Inalienable rights series ; bk. 3)
Includes bibliographical references.
ISBN 978-0-19-530424-4
1. Firearms—Law and legislation—United States.   2. Gun control—United
States.   3. United States. Constitution. 2nd Amendment.   I. Title.
KF3941.T87   2007
344.7305'33—DC22
2007011748

1 3 5 7 9 8 6 4 2
Printed in the United States of America
on acid-free paper

For Leonard

Contents

. . .

CONTENTS

Editor's Note

. . .

We hold these truths to be self-evident, that all men are created equal, that they are endowed by their Creator with certain unalienable Rights....

—THE DECLARATION OF INDEPENDENCE

. . .

This is the third volume in this series on Inalienable Rights. The first, Richard Posner's *Not a Suicide Pact: The Constitution in Time of National Emergency*, explored the constitutional issues posed by such controversial policies as detention, torture, and electronic surveillance during the war on terrorism. The second, Michael Klarman's *Unfinished Business: Racial Equality in American History*, addressed the constitutional challenge presented by the issue of race. Here, in the wake of the mass killing at Virginia Tech that has prompted the latest paroxysm of national self-examination, Mark Tushnet takes on the vexing question of guns and the Constitution.

The Second Amendment states, "A well regulated Militia, being necessary to the security of a free State, the right of the people to keep and bear Arms, shall not be infringed." What does this mean? May the government prohibit all sales of handguns? May it prohibit the private ownership of bazookas? May it require all persons who want to own a gun to take and pass a test similar to a driver's test?

In *Out of Range: Why the Constitution Can't End the Battle over Guns*, Tushnet considers the competing interpretations of the Second Amendment. He addresses both the strictly "originalist" approach, which on balance supports an individual right to possess guns, and the more traditional and more eclectic approach, which on balance supports a more collective view of the right and therefore allows for greater government regulation. By exploring these different methodologies, he sheds light not only on the Second Amendment but more broadly on the process of constitutional interpretation.

Because Tushnet finds both approaches and both interpretations plausible, he suggests that there may be no "neutral" way to resolve the dilemma. He notes, though, that there is a close correlation between the interpretive approaches individuals favor and their policy preferences about gun control. Those who favor gun control tend to embrace the traditional approach to interpretation of the Second Amendment; those who oppose gun control tend to endorse the originalist approach. In short, policy preferences seem to determine constitutional analyses.

He then turns to social science research about the effects of different gun policies, ranging from "must issue" laws that authorize individuals to carry concealed weapons to bans on the sale of handguns. After considering the research, Tushnet again concludes that the data are inconclusive, but that proponents of the competing views of the Second Amendment tend to accept the studies that support their own policy preferences and to discredit the studies that undermine their preferences.

Tushnet suggests that this tells us a lot about both law and politics. Specifically, he argues that our views on guns have less to do with our views of the Constitution or our views on public safety than with our views about who we want to be as a nation. The dispute over guns, he concludes, is part of the "culture wars" and must realistically be so understood. If this is right, then no amount of argument about the meaning of the Constitution and no amount of evidence about the effects of various gun laws will persuade most people that they are "wrong." Something deeper and more fundamental is at stake.

True to the mission of this series, this is a provocative and disturbing thesis. It raises profound question about the way we make decisions both as individuals and as a society.

April 2007   Geoffrey R. Stone

Introduction

. . .

A PHOTO OF John Kerry fully decked out in camouflage gear and carrying a 12-gauge shotgun was not something most Americans expected to see in their morning paper in late October 2004. But with the election two weeks away, Kerry and his handlers must have found irresistible a photo op with Kerry returning from duck-hunting after having "bagged four geese." Politically astute observers understood that Kerry was attempting to inoculate himself against charges that he and his party were "anti-gun." Credibility with gun-rights supporters in the "red states" that Bush had carried in 2000 mattered a lot to Kerry's prospects. The photo didn't help, though. The National Rifle Association's political fund immediately bought an ad saying, "If John Kerry thinks the Second Amendment is about photo ops, he's daffy.... If John Kerry wins, hunters lose."

In one of the Gore-Bush debates, Gore had listed a number of new gun-control policies he hoped to see adopted, while George W. Bush stressed that violence was "really a matter of culture."

The cultural division over gun policy matters politically. Commentators attributed Al Gore's losses in the 2000 elections in Arkansas, West Virginia, and Tennessee to his——and more particularly his party's—perceived position on gun control: Enough voters who otherwise would have voted for Gore, they believe, decided against doing so primarily because they were worried about what a Gore administration would do about guns.

Gun control and gun rights have become important components of the battle between "blue states" favoring gun control and "red states" favoring gun rights. But, as we will see, the battles are about more than mere politics. Responding to the Kerry photo op, a Bush spokesman said, the event was "another example of John Kerry presenting himself as someone he is not." Even though who John Kerry really was might seem far removed from questions about gun policy, the Bush campaign's statement captured a deep truth about our current debates over gun policy. Disagreements over the Second Amendment and its meaning are no longer fought on legal and policy grounds alone. Disputes over gun policy have become deeply enmeshed in the *culture* wars between liberals and conservatives, between people who live in cities and people who live in the country. The Second Amendment is one of the arenas in which we as Americans try to figure out who we are.

Culture war battles, particularly about the law, have a stylized form. Partisans are quite convinced that their interpretation of the Constitution is the only one a reasonable person could come up with—and so their opponents must be unreasonable. They are convinced that empirical evidence supports the common-sense conclusions they already have reached: Jane supports the adoption of laws allowing more people to carry concealed weapons, because *of course* criminals will be deterred if they don't know whether their intended victim has a gun; Greg supports the adoption of laws requiring the "safe storage" of guns, because *of course* having guns lying around means that lots of people will be killed accidentally. As we'll see, the culture wars have produced competing incompatible stories—about the original understanding of the Second Amendment, about how the Supreme Court has interpreted the amendment, about gun policy—each of which is thought to be unshakably true by its adherents.

Neutrality is probably impossible in a culture wars battle. Even to stand apart from a particular battle is to take a position. So, I should be as clear as I can about my commitments and conclusions. Before writing this book, I had only an academic interest in the Second Amendment—and I still do; neither the Second Amendment nor gun policy generally ranks high on my list of concerns. Some interesting articles on the Second Amendment had been written—outnumbered, of course, by the ones that simply repeated the talking points familiar from both sides. Reviewing the legal literature, I've concluded that no one has really knock-down arguments for their positions.

Nelson Lund is now the Patrick Henry Professor of Constitutional Law and the Second Amendment at George Mason University's law school. A few years before receiving that honor, Lund wrote that determining the correct interpretation of the Second Amendment was "not a hard or a close question." Anyone who tells you that is blowing smoke. More accurate was the observation of one of the country's most respected scholars of constitutional law, William Van Alstyne, that "no provision in the Constitution causes one to stumble quite so much on a first reading, or second, or third reading."

Here's what I've concluded.

• As with many constitutional provisions, there's no definitive answer to what the Second Amendment means. And arguments over its meaning are affected, for the worse, by their ties to

[xv]

the culture wars. The arguments demonstrate the validity of what students of the Internet have called Godwin's Law (named after the Internet guru who first described it): As discussion proceeds, the probability that one's adversaries will be likened to Nazis and that Hitler will be invoked approaches one very quickly. Proponents of the right to own guns for personal use are "gun nuts" or "insurrectionists" to their opponents; proponents of gun control are fascists or socialists to theirs. A distinguished federal judge invokes the Holocaust and the Third Reich in criticizing gun control; gun-rights proponents title an article, "Of Holocausts and Gun Control." The terminology is so contested that I have adopted the awkward phrases "proponents of gun rights" and "proponents of gun control" to describe the contending sides, in an effort to achieve some degree of neutrality.

- As I read the legal materials, the arguments about the Second Amendment's meaning are in reasonably close balance. Looking to an understanding of its terms when it was adopted, I conclude in Chapters 1 and 2 that the pro–gun-rights position is a bit stronger than the alternative. But looking to all the other components that go into good legal arguments, I conclude in Chapter 3 that the pro–gun-control position is significantly stronger than the alternative. That chapter turns to the other considerations— particularly, Supreme Court precedents—that ordinarily are part of constitutional interpretation. In the end, the gun-control story is slightly, but only slightly, better than the gun-rights one—a conclusion that is unlikely to comfort either side. And substantial amounts of gun control are constitutionally permissible even if we accept the best versions of the arguments favored by gun-rights proponents.

- To understand the debate over gun rights and gun control, we have to examine public policy as well as law. Chapter 4 turns to the public policy issues that are inevitably part of the debate over the Second Amendment. Here the evidence seems pretty clear that any gun-related policy likely to survive a political process deeply affected by the culture wars will not do much to reduce violence. Making it somewhat harder to buy guns by regulating sales not simply at gun stores but at gun shows won't make much difference; neither will barring the police from confiscating guns during weather catastrophes like Hurricane Katrina. The sources of violence are deeply rooted enough in culture and psychology that adding or dropping specific gun-control regulations is quite unlikely to make much difference. Perhaps paradoxically, advocates of gun control might actually be impeding the adoption of more effective policies for reducing violence. The reason is that when gun control becomes politically important, a battle in the culture wars occurs. Even when advocates of gun control win such battles, they typically find it difficult to enact or sustain strong gun-control policies. An example: Getting more cops on the streets is pretty clearly the best crime-control policy that's come down the pike over the past decades. And Bill Clinton did manage to persuade Congress to help finance 100,000 more police officers. The same Congress, though, devoted a lot of effort to enacting the Brady Bill, requiring background checks on gun purchasers. Gun-rights proponents hated the Brady Bill, and their mobilization against its supporters helped fuel the Republican takeover of Congress in 1994—after which federal financial support for more cops on the streets evaporated.

• Of course, often gun-control proponents lose the political battles. Take the issue of gun control off the political agenda, and those interested in reducing violence might win more elections—and then enact anti-violence policies other than gun control that might actually accomplish something.

• Bad arguments are quite common. Consider the response of some gun-control proponents to the argument that the Second Amendment protects the right to keep and bear arms to ensure that an armed people will be able to resist an oppressive government. That argument is, as we will see, a substantial one. But, opponents say, how could *the Constitution* protect a right to resist authority created by the Constitution itself? The Second Amendment, they say, certainly couldn't have been designed to license treason, or even to embed in the Constitution a pre-constitutional or natural right to resist tyranny. To which one reasonable response is: Why not? There's nothing peculiar about embedding a pre-constitutional natural right in the Constitution; indeed, liberals like the idea of invoking the Ninth Amendment, which seems to assert that the people have some natural rights not spelled out in the Constitution, as the basis for recognizing a constitutional right to privacy. (And, even more ironically for those liberals, the natural-rights argument might find support for gun rights in that same Ninth Amendment, which might be interpreted to guarantee a natural right of self-defense, rendering all the dithering over the details of Second Amendment history pointless.) Gun-control proponents have good arguments on their side, but their outrage at claims for a right to resist an oppressive government with arms isn't one of them.

• The bad argument on the side of those who oppose substantial restrictions on the right to own guns is at the heart of the gun-rights case: Gun-rights proponents proceed as if their position would be unassailable were they to show that people in 1791, when the Second Amendment was adopted, understood its words to guarantee a right in every person to own a weapon for personal use. Constitutional law doesn't work that way, though. Arguments based on original understanding are important, but for at least a century and probably longer they have never been the be-all-and-end-all of constitutional discussion.

Like all battles in culture wars, then, the fights over the Second Amendment are really about something else—not about what the Second Amendment means, or about how to reduce violence, but, as hinted by the Bush spokesman's comment about John Kerry's duck-hunting, about how we understand ourselves as Americans. Get that straight, and the fights over the Second Amendment would go away. But, of course, we *can't* get our national self-understanding straight, because we are always trying to figure out who we are, and revising our self-understandings. And so the battle over the Second Amendment will continue.

CHAPTER ONE

The Standard Model and the Original Understanding

GEORGE W. BUSH'S victory in 2000 was also a victory for gun-rights proponents and for originalists. Bush's attorney general John Ashcroft took office with an agenda that included changing the Department of Justice's position on the Second Amendment. To this end, Ashcroft charged the Office of Legal Counsel (OLC), which acts as the attorney general's lawyer, with the task of producing a comprehensive analysis of the Second Amendment. Stephen Bradbury, formerly a law clerk to Justice Clarence Thomas and later nominated to head OLC after the turmoil occasioned by the release of the so-called Torture Memos, took on the job of producing the memorandum. The 106-page document stated its conclusion on its cover: "The Second Amendment secures a right of individuals generally, not a right of State or a right restricted to persons serving in militias." The OLC memorandum on the Second Amendment, which helps shape the government's position in gun cases, can serve as our guide to the Second Amendment's meaning.

What, though, does it mean to say that the Second Amendment "secures a right of individuals"? Consider this policy proposal, which I'll use throughout this book: Before you can buy a gun, you have to take a licensing test, just as you have to take a driving test before you can drive a car. Canada's Firearms Act, adopted in 1995, has a test requirement. (It also requires gun registration, which isn't part of the proposal I'm imagining here: Gun-rights proponents worry that registration is the first step toward confiscation, or at least gives the government a list of gun owners it could use if it wanted to confiscate guns.) The test has two parts. The first is a written, multiple-choice exam, asking questions about your knowledge of guns—their parts, how they work, what ammunition fits different guns—and about how to handle guns safely. A sample question shows a pistol's sights and asks if they are properly aligned. Another asks whether you can use rimfire ammunition in a center-fire firearm. The other part is like the street-driving part of a driver's test: You have to handle different types of firearms under different conditions—using a rifle in a field, firing a handgun on a firing range. Does requiring that you pass this test violate your "individual right" to keep and bear arms?

The answer depends, of course, on two things: Does the Second Amendment protect an individual right, as the Department of Justice memo concluded? And if it does, exactly what kinds of regulations are prohibited by the amendment? And those questions, in turn, depend on how we interpret the Second Amendment.

How do we go about interpreting the Constitution? Of course we begin with the text; as we'll see, the Second Amendment's words don't tell us enough about what it means. Texts alone almost never resolve constitutional controversies. Nobody who thinks seriously about the Constitution thinks that the First

Amendment's statement that "Congress shall make no law... abridging the freedom of speech" in itself tells us that Congress has no power to regulate the distribution of pornography over the Internet. We have to do some additional work of interpretation to figure out whether Congress has that power.

To resolve uncertainties, we often turn next to the way the words were understood at the time they were written—an inquiry usually described as *originalist*. To continue with the First Amendment: In 1791 no one could have known about the Internet or about modern forms of pornography, so the originalist inquiry isn't going to be all that helpful. What next? If we remain unsure of the provision's meaning we look to the way the provision fits into some overall account of why we have a Constitution. We might think that the First Amendment is aimed at ensuring that we have complete freedom to discuss public affairs, in which case Congress might have the power to regulate Internet pornography, or we might think that it is aimed at protecting everyone's ability freely to think about whatever he or she finds important, in which case Congress might not have that power. Typically, we look to the way courts have interpreted the provision over the decades to find out which account of the Constitution fits better with our national experience.

Over the past twenty years, gun-rights proponents have transformed the academic understanding of the Second Amendment. Their originalist account has become known as the "Standard Model," signaling both that it has gained widespread acceptance and that the earlier, more gun-control friendly interpretation now has been pushed to the margins. The Standard Model is generally described as an "individual rights" account of the Second Amendment. But even though it's referred to as a single model, the "individual rights" account actually comes in three distinct flavors.

- The *pure* individual-rights model: The right to keep and bear arms is just like all the other rights in the Bill of Rights—held by each of us as an individual, to be exercised for whatever reasons each of us might have (recreation, self-defense, whatever), and subject only to rather limited forms of government regulation when there's some truly pressing social need served by the regulation. This is the purest variant—leading to great suspicion of extensive programs for registering handguns or for regulating when and to whom guns can be sold.

- A *citizen-militia* individual right: The right is held by each of us as an individual, but for reasons related to the maintenance of a militia, understood not as the state-organized National Guard but as the term *militia* was understood when the Second Amendment was adopted—the entire body of the people organized *on their own* to ensure that the government remains faithful to our national principles. Here the focus is on the possibility that gun owners can get together to resist an oppressive government, just as the American revolutionaries did in 1776. As with the pure individual-rights variant, this one too worries about registration programs, because they make it possible for the government to locate and disarm the very people who might oppose its depredations.

- A *citizen-related* individual right: The right might include the citizen-militia right, but goes beyond it so that each of us has a right and indeed a duty to keep and bear arms for purposes of self-defense when the government fails to perform its side of the social contract and protect us against criminals who would deprive us of our life, liberty, or property. This variant is particularly concerned about restrictions on gun ownership—requirements that guns be locked away when they are not in use, for example—that might make it hard for people to defend themselves against criminals.

The OLC memorandum on the Second Amendment endorsed the Standard Model. That model's analysis of original understanding is frequently taken to support the pure individual right. Actually, it is more compatible with the militia- or citizen-related individual right, and the OLC memorandum doesn't choose among the possibilities. The practical effect of the difference is that, properly understood, the Standard Model allows at least a bit more government regulation than proponents of a strong, pure individual right to keep and bear arms think permissible.

The pure individual-rights account starts with the observation that the Second Amendment is, well, part of the Bill of *Rights*. Everything else in the Bill of Rights is an individual right, and it makes sense to treat the right to keep and bear arms just like the freedom of speech or the privilege against compelled self-incrimination—a right that anyone can exercise for any reason at all, whether the rest of us view the reasons as good, bad, or indifferent. Of course, governments can limit our rights under some circumstances, which we'll examine in Chapter 2, but the individual-rights view says that government regulations of the right to keep and bear arms have to be justified in just the same way that we justify restrictions on free speech.

Simple enough, but there are two points about the Second Amendment's text that might give us pause. Here's what the Second Amendment says: "A well regulated Militia, being necessary to the security of a free State, the right of the people to keep and bear Arms, shall not be infringed." The phrase including the term "well-regulated Militia" is usually called the Second Amendment's preamble.

The first point about the text is this: The right is described as a right "of the people." That's an unusual formulation within the Bill of Rights. The right of free speech isn't described as a right "of the people," nor is the privilege against compelled self-incrimination. The second point is the amendment's preamble.

The phrase "the people" occurs in three other provisions in the first ten amendments, and in each it gives the right a somewhat "collectivist" tinge: The phrase helps describe a right that is somehow associated with people acting together. The Ninth Amendment says that listing certain rights in the Constitution "shall not be construed to deny or disparage others retained *by the people*." Judge Robert Bork notoriously described the Ninth Amendment as something like an ink-blot on the Constitution—a set of words so obscure that it is impossible to interpret. People have tried, though, and one candidate is that the rights retained "by the people" are rights found in *state* constitutions but not in the Bill of Rights. That probably isn't the best interpretation of the Ninth Amendment, but it does suggest that using the term "the people" in the Constitution might signal that we're dealing with a special kind of right.

The Fourth Amendment refers to "the right *of the people* to be secure in their persons, houses, papers, and effects." Here the Supreme Court has suggested that the term refers to an organized community. When a Mexican citizen challenged as illegal a search of his Mexican home conducted by U.S. law enforcement agents, Chief Justice William Rehnquist wrote for a majority that foreign nationals living abroad weren't protected by the Fourth Amendment, because the amendment protected only "the people" of—or in—the United States. Chief Justice Rehnquist thought the textual point suggestive: When the Constitution used the term *the people*, it pointed our attention to "*a class of persons* who are part of a national community."

The First Amendment also refers to "the people," not in connection with free speech itself but in describing "the right of the people peaceably to assemble, and to petition the Government for a redress of grievances." Even more obviously than with the other provisions, this one refers to a right that almost inherently has to be exercised by a group of people.

As Chief Justice Rehnquist put it in the decision dealing with the search in Mexico, these textual points are "by no means conclusive." And, indeed, we shouldn't make too much of the description of the right to keep and bear arms as one held by "the people." The rights picked out by that phrase might be rights *distributed* to each of us as individuals. We then choose whether and how to exercise our right to assemble, for example. As the OLC memorandum put it, " 'the people' might choose to exercise those individual rights in groups rather than alone,... but that does not make their rights 'collective'... in the sense of depending on the will or actions of a State."

The individual-rights view builds on a powerful account of what the OLC memorandum calls the "structure" of the Bill of Rights. The right to keep and bear arms has a slightly more community-oriented flavor than most of the other rights in the Bill of Rights, but in the end, it's more similar to than different from them. At least to this point, it's an individual right. What about the structure of the Second Amendment itself? Before we examine the amendment's preamble, observe what right the amendment protects: a right "to keep and bear arms." When used separately in the eighteenth century, "keep" and "bear" had their ordinary meanings—you could keep a weapon in your house, and then you'd bear it outside. When used together, though, the meaning was more restricted. The evidence is overwhelming that "keep and bear" was a technical phrase whose terms traveled together, like "cease and desist" or "hue and cry." "Keep and bear" referred to weapons in connection with military uses, even when the terms used separately might refer to hunting or other activities. This pushes in the direction of a military-oriented interpretation of the amendment.

So does the other thing that leaps out from the Second Amendment's text—the preamble's reference to the "well regulated Militia." Gun-rights proponents take the preamble to support what I've called a militia-oriented individual-rights interpretation. We have the right to keep and bear arms because doing so is somehow helpful in sustaining a well-regulated militia—although a lot will turn on what we understand such a militia to be.

Only one other provision of the national constitution has a similar preamble. The copyright and patents clause gives Congress the power "to promote the Progress of Science and useful Arts, by securing for limited Times to Authors and Inventors the exclusive Right to their respective Writings and Discoveries." Do these preambles *limit* the scope of the provisions, placing some conditions on when the right comes into play, or merely *explain* why they are in the Constitution? Two gun-control proponents describe the difference in this way: Suppose we had a constitutional provision, "Commerce within and between the several States being essential to the economy of the Nation, the right of the people to breed and keep horses shall not be infringed." If the preamble is merely an explanation, it wouldn't matter that horses are no longer essential to ensuring the nation's economic success; we'd still have a right to breed and keep horses for recreational riding, plowing the fields, or anything else. But if the preamble is a limitation on the right's scope, legislatures could limit an individual's right to breed and keep horses to occasions when doing so was essential for the nation's economy—which is to say, never.

Gun-control proponents say that the Second Amendment's preamble operates as a limitation or condition: People have a right to keep weapons only in connection with their participation in the militia—and in a "well regulated" militia at that. For gun-control proponents, that militia is, today, the state-run National Guard. It follows for them that legislatures can regulate gun ownership however they want: Legislatures impose limitations on gun ownership for people who are members of the National Guard, as part of their effort to regulate the militia well, and people who are not members of the National Guard have no rights under the Second Amendment.

Even if the preamble *is* a limitation, we still need to know what a well-regulated militia is. Is today's National Guard the militia the preamble refers to? Maybe not. The text, after all, refers to a right of "the people" generally, not the rights of people in state-organized militias. Indeed, some early state constitutions also included a guarantee of a right to bear arms, protected against state regulation. For example, Kentucky's 1792 Constitution provided that "the right of the citizens to bear arms in defense of themselves and the State shall not be questioned." *That* provision, and similar ones, couldn't possibly apply only to members of the state-organized militia. Note, though, as another indication of how convoluted the arguments can get, that the Kentucky provision uses only the word *bear* and not the military-related phrase *keep and bear*.

All this turns on the proposition that the Second Amendment's preamble operates as a limitation. But that's not the only possibility. State constitutions adopted in the 1780s and 1790s have provisions with preambles too. The New Hampshire Constitution of 1784, for example, says this: "The Liberty of the Press is essential to the security of freedom in a state; it ought, therefore, to be inviolably preserved." Here the preamble is clearly an explanation, not a limitation: You couldn't defend prosecuting a newspaper for libel by showing that the story it published didn't have anything to do with ensuring freedom in the state. The individual-rights interpretation of the Second Amendment is pretty clearly strengthened if the preamble explains but doesn't limit the right the rest of the amendment describes.

How does the preamble *explain* the substantive right created in the Second Amendment's second half? The originalist materials indicate that the term *militia* might well have been understood in the 1790s to refer to the entire body of the people. A typical phrasing came in the constitutional amendment proposed by the convention called in Virginia to ratify the Constitution: "that the people have the right to keep and bear arms; that a well regulated militia composed of the body of the people trained to arms is the proper, natural and safe defence of a free state." *The body of the people*: The militia consisted of *every* able-bodied mature white male. It was not an organization with a list of qualifications for membership, or indeed any sort of "organization" at all. The militia was identical to the people (subject, of course, to race and gender restrictions that don't have any bearing on explaining why the people have a right to keep and bear arms). That's why the militia-related right is fairly described as an individual right held by everyone, not limited to people who are members of the state-organized National Guard.

As a matter of original understanding, this interpretation seems unassailable. The best gun-control proponents can do with the founding era's equation of the militia with the body of the people is to demonstrate, somehow, that times change, and that the Second Amendment's reference to a well-regulated militia now points to the state-organized militia, not the body of the people. Doing so, though, moves outside the originalist framework, because it implies that as times change, so do meanings—which is exactly what originalism denies.

The Virginia proposal also helps explain the individual right through its reference to the "defence of a free people," transformed in the Second Amendment into "the security of a free State." The originalist argument draws on pre-Revolutionary history in Great Britain and the colonies to give meaning to this phrase. Those who lived in the founding era drew important lessons from their understanding of British and colonial history. The political theorists on whom that generation drew began with a general account of the relation between the people and their government, then turned to questions about what to do when things worked out badly—that is, when a government failed to provide security for a free people.

Historians have struggled to figure out the precise contours of the political theories on which the framing generation drew. I greatly oversimplify in saying that the prevailing theory blended strains of liberal individualism, associated in political theory with the Englishman John Locke, and a tradition of civic republicanism whose greatest expositor was the Italian Nicolo Machiavelli. For these thinkers, the point of government was to provide security for a free people. The earlier author, Machiavelli, emphasized the importance of physical security against external attack and internal subversion. A permanent and professional—"standing"—army might provide physical security, but it too easily could undermine freedom. Civic republicans instead looked to an alert—and armed—citizenry for defense. People devoted to their nation would voluntarily take up arms in its defense.

Locke and more individualist thinkers expanded on the idea of an alert citizenry. They argued that citizens could protect their liberty more directly by participating in daily government. Locke and his intellectual heirs were the great modern theorists of *representative* government: Government was needed to provide security, and representation was needed to keep government in line. In the United States, the founding generation deepened this theory by offering a complex account of how different government institutions might check each other.

By the time of the Constitution's framing, the prevailing political theory offered two remedies for government failures in providing security for a free people.

- *Representative government.* Governments started to oppress the people when they weren't under popular control. No one chose the kings who exercised unlimited power. The British parliament had two houses, one hereditary and one elected, but the elected House of Commons had become corrupted, meaning, to the founding generation, that it had become dependent on the king rather than on the people. The American Revolution aimed at establishing representative government and thereby reducing the risk of government tyranny.

- A *right of armed resistance.* Even a representative government might become corrupt, though. Elected officials might decide to line their own pockets. Their control over the army would allow them to carry out their schemes, perhaps even to the point of stopping people from voting or stopping the true representatives of the people from taking the seats they were entitled to in the legislature. The remedy? Armed resistance to oppression by the people. The Declaration of Independence invoked the right of armed resistance when it referred to "the Right of the People to alter or to abolish" a government that became "destructive" of the ends for which governments were created. And precisely because this was a right of armed resistance against the government, it could not be carried out under the auspices of the government itself. Rather, the people, organizing themselves by choosing their own leaders, would resist the government.

The Constitution and the Second Amendment combined these mechanisms to defend a free people. There was a problem with the Constitution, though. True, it created a representative government. But during and just after the Revolution, the new nation needed a government was that reasonably powerful, particularly so that it could take its place on the international stage. The weak government that existed from 1776 to 1789 was unable to enforce treaty obligations, for example, which placed the nation at risk. The proposed Constitution would create a government with enough power to advance national goals, to be sure, but for exactly that reason the government posed a risk of oppression.

The risk of government abuse of power was exacerbated by the drafters' insistence on creating a national armed force. One of the charges leveled against George III in the Declaration of Independence was that he had "kept among us, in Times of Peace, Standing Armies, without the consent of our Legislatures." And even though the creation of a representative government would give "consent" to keeping permanent armed forces, concern about the possibility that corrupt leaders would use standing armies to oppress the people persisted. Yet George Washington prodded the drafters to create an effective national army, drawing on his experience as the leader of the revolutionary army—and on the prestige he had gained. Washington believed that the new nation could not succeed without a significant armed force. The Constitution's drafters agreed, but they also understood that lots of people continued to fear an overly strong national government. Acknowledging that concern, they gave Congress the power to "raise and support Armies," but immediately qualified that power: "no Appropriation of Money to that Use shall be for a longer Term than two Years."

Armies were good for meeting threats from abroad, but they might be a problem if turned inward. The Constitution's drafters tried to keep the armed forces focused outward by providing a different means for dealing with domestic disorder or insurgency. They acknowledged that the body of the people could constitute a militia by giving Congress two powers. It could "provide for calling forth the Militia to execute the Laws of the Union, suppress Insurrections, and repel Invasions." It also could "provide for organizing, arming, and disciplining the Militia," and for "governing" the militia when it was called into national service.

These provisions assume that there *was* a militia, but taken alone, they seem to give Congress essentially complete control over both the national army and the militia. That would defeat the purpose of placing some limits on the use of armed force *against* the people. So the Constitution created a counterweight to congressional power: The states would have the power to appoint officers of the militia, and would implement Congress's plans for training militia members. The thought here was that state-appointed officers might disregard orders coming from an oppressive government, whereas officers appointed by the national government would not.

Does the Constitution's recognition of state authority to appoint militia officers show that the Second Amendment's preamble refers to a state-organized militia? Not necessarily. The original Constitution's provisions dealing with militias certainly do lean in that direction. But these provisions implicitly distinguish between the full militia, consisting of the body of the people, and a select militia, organized by the states. Congress has the power to direct how the select militia should be trained, and can call *it* into national service. In contrast, the Second Amendment refers solely to the militia understood as the body of the people.

This interpretation is defensible, but it's something of a stretch. Reading the Second Amendment against the background of the original Constitution's references to the militia, we might conclude that the Second Amendment's preamble refers to the state-organized militia. But of course, as long as that reference is simply an explanation and not a condition, this textual point doesn't really weaken the Standard Model.

As the Constitution emerged from the Philadelphia Convention, it attempted to combine a reasonably powerful representative national government with mechanisms for keeping that government under some threat of armed resistance. Adopting the Constitution was not a sure thing, though. Its opponents, called anti-Federalists, worried that the new government would be *too* powerful. They opposed adopting the Constitution in its original form, and proposed a raft of amendments that would make the new government more acceptable to them. Among the more common proposals were those guaranteeing a right to keep and bear arms. The pro-Constitution forces argued that the Constitution didn't need improving. As a fallback, they urged ratification, to be followed by the consideration of specific amendments. That's what happened.

The Second Amendment reflects the view that the combination of representative government with some modest limits on the size of the armed forces under national control in the original Constitution didn't do enough to reduce the risk of government oppression. Gun-rights proponents take the amendment to put the right of armed resistance—the right to keep and bear arms for the defense of a free people—into the Constitution.

That's the basic story. Now, for some of the specific statements from the founding era (and before and after). After setting out a quotation, I'll give you the Standard Model's interpretation—and, sometimes, what gun-control proponents have to say about the quotation, to give you a flavor of the debate.

THE BRITISH DECLARATION OF RIGHTS (1689)

During the mid-1600s, England boiled over with religious and political controversy. After a brief period of popular rule, the monarchy was restored in 1660. The new king, Charles II, expanded the select militia into a standing army, and his parliament passed the "Game Act" of 1671, which prohibited anyone other than a small elite from owning a gun. When James II, a Catholic, took the throne in 1685, he disarmed the Protestant militia in Ireland and aggressively enforced the Game Act against his political opponents.

Those opponents relied on the armed citizenry for support and installed William and Mary of Orange on the throne in the Glorious Revolution of 1688. The new parliament celebrated its victory in the Declaration of Rights, adopted in February 1689. Like the colonists' Declaration of Independence almost a century later, the Declaration of Rights had two parts, a list of grievances and a list of rights. Among the grievances were "raising and keeping a standing Army," and "causing several good subjects, being protestants, to be disarmed, at the same time when papists were both armed and employed, contrary to law." The parallel rights were these: "That the raising or keeping a standing Army within the Kingdom in time of Peace, unless it be with the Consent of Parliament, is against Law," and "That the Subjects which are Protestants, may have Arms for their Defence suitable to their Condition, and as allowed by Law."

The OLC memorandum says that the latter article "set out a personal right." A draft of the Declaration said, "the subjects, which are Protestants, should provide and keep arms for the common defence." The final document shifts the term from "common defense" to "their defense," underlining that the Declaration protects an individual right.

But don't the restriction of the right to Protestants and the recognition that they have whatever rights they do only "as allowed by law" show that the Declaration of Rights provides little support for an expansive vision of gun rights? Not according to the OLC memo. Those restrictions, it argues, go to the scope of the right, but don't weaken the claim that whatever rights there are, are held by individuals personally, and not in connection with militia membership. In England, with its tradition of parliamentary supremacy, of course any rights were subject to statutory regulation. But the OLC memo continues, "That characteristic of English rights hardly prevented Americans from borrowing and adapting them to a different constitutional structure."

WILLIAM BLACKSTONE

William Blackstone, professor of law at Oxford University in the 1760s, published an enormously influential four-volume description and defense of British law, the *Commentaries on the Laws of England* (1765–69). Americans regularly referred to Blackstone's *Commentaries* when they tried to identify the rights they had as Englishmen—rights, they argued, that were being denied them as colonists. The *Commentaries* were a detailed exposition, category by category, of English law. They began with a description of the relation between individual rights and the purposes of government. Everyone had what Blackstone called "absolute rights," even in the state of nature. These rights could be reduced to the rights of personal security, personal liberty, and private property.

Following the standard political theory of the time, Blackstone observed, "the principal view of human laws is, or ought always to be, to explain, protect, and enforce" these rights. But simply *saying* that you had these basic rights didn't guarantee that you would enjoy them. And, Blackstone said with some satisfaction, British law did more. It provided the rights with what he called "auxiliary" rights that "serve principally as barriers to protect and maintain inviolate the three great and primary rights." What were these? The organization of Parliament and limitations on the King's prerogative (which, we might say, reappeared in the United States as the guarantees of liberty provided by representative government). Then the right to "apply[] to the courts of justice for redress of injuries." Fourth, if the courts failed, the right to petition parliament for a redress of grievances (which reappeared in the First Amendment).

And finally, the fifth auxiliary right: "that of having arms for their defence, suitable to their condition and degree, and such as are allowed by law, [which is]...indeed a public allowance, under due restrictions, of the natural right of resistance and self-preservation, when the sanctions of society and laws are found insufficient to restrain the violence of oppression." According to OLC, this treats the right to bear arms as tied to "the natural—and thus individual and pre-political—right of self-defense." And, OLC continues, Blackstone does not mention the militia at all in this initial exposition of basic rights.

Blackstone supports the individual-rights view, then, because he treats the right to bear arms as an aspect of "resistance and self-preservation"—to resist an oppressive government and to protect your basic rights when government fails to do so.

THE PENNSYLVANIA "MINORITY REPORT"

The anti-Federalists who opposed adopting the Constitution began to organize soon after the draft was submitted to the states for ratification. Delaware ratified quickly, and unanimously. Next came Pennsylvania, where ratification was hard-fought. Pennsylvania had the most democratic government in the nation from the Revolution to the adoption of the Constitution, and many of its most ardent democrats were deeply suspicious of what they saw as the aristocratic tendencies in the proposed national constitution. The state's voters chose a majority of pro-ratification delegates, but the anti-Federalists were well-represented. Street battles broke out in Philadelphia, and anti-Federalists tried to deprive the ratification convention of a quorum by staying away from its meetings. Eventually they were rounded up and forced into the hall.

The Pennsylvania convention voted to ratify by a margin of 46 to 23. The dissenting delegates published a "Minority Report" outlining their objections, including the absence of a Bill of Rights. Their pamphlet listed amendments they had proposed but that the majority had rejected. One drew on the 1776 state Declaration of Rights:

> That the people have a right to bear arms for the defence of themselves and their own State, or the United States, or for the purpose of killing game; and no law shall be passed for disarming the people or any of them, unless for crimes committed, or real danger of public injury from individuals; and as standing armies in the time of peace are dangerous to liberty, they ought not to be kept up; and that the military shall be kept under strict subordination to and be governed by the civil power.

As with the state's own provision, this proposal, especially with its reference to "killing game," disconnects the right to bear arms from any military purposes. The Pennsylvania Minority Report shows that those who insisted on including the Second Amendment in the Bill of Rights understood the right to bear arms to be an individual one.

Garry Wills vigorously attacked the Standard Model's reliance on the Minority Report. To Wills, the Report was "an omnium gatherum of arguments against the Constitution," whose prime mover was a now obscure anti-Federalist named Robert Whitehill. As Wills tells the story, Whitehill proposed fifteen amendments, not as serious policy options but simply to block ratification. Wills describes one proposal as a "wild[] objection to the Constitution...surely not backed by others in the minority." Among the proposals in "his throw-in-the-kitchen-sink approach" was the provision on the right to bear arms. Wills parses the proposal, writing that Whitehill "is a desperate man..., unable to make his own motion coherently enough for the convention to understand it." Wills concludes, "It is a sign of the desperation of the Standard Modelers that they take these ill-conceived phrases of Whitehill as the deliberated position of a whole 'minority,' and want to make *them* the text that controls our interpretation of 'near arms' in the Second Amendment.... Did even Whitehill mean what he was saying? Or,... was he just babbling to head off the impending vote?"

This is certainly fun to read, but is it accurate? Partly so. No one has challenged Wills's account of where the Minority Report came from, or his description of Whitehill's efforts. The problem, though, is that, whatever Wills thinks of Whitehill's competence, the Minority Report was "widely circulated" and "influential." Historian Saul Cornell writes that the Minority Report "attained a semi-official status." So, whatever its provenance, the Minority Report—and its individual-right theme—has to be counted as part of the Second Amendment's background.

JOSEPH STORY

Supreme Court Justice Joseph Story was the American Blackstone. Appointed to the Supreme Court in 1811, when he was only thirty-two years old (a youth record that still stands), Story also taught at Harvard Law School, and wrote—and wrote, and wrote. Among his many books was the influential *Commentaries on the Constitution of the United States*, published in 1833. This is of course long after the Second Amendment was adopted and strictly speaking doesn't tell us much about what the original understanding was. But Story was at least close to the founding generation, and his prestige as an early interpreter is enormous. So what Story had to say is often taken to be a pretty good indication of original understanding.

After devoting twenty pages to the First Amendment, Story had two paragraphs on the Second:

> The importance of this article will scarcely be doubted by any persons, who have duly reflected upon the subject. The militia is the natural defence of a free country against sudden foreign invasions, domestic insurrections, and domestic usurpations of power by rulers. It is against sound policy for a free people to keep up large military establishments and standing armies in time of peace, both from the enormous expenses, with which they are attended, and the facile means, which they afford to ambitious and unprincipled rulers, to subvert the government, or trample upon the rights of the people. The right of the citizens to keep and bear arms has justly been considered, as the palladium of the liberties of a republic; since it offers a strong moral check against the usurpation and arbitrary power of rulers; and will generally, even if these are successful in the first instance, enable the people to resist and triumph over them. And yet, though this truth would seem so clear, and the importance of a well regulated militia would seem so undeniable, it cannot be disguised, that among the American people there is a growing indifference to any system of militia discipline, and a strong disposition, from a sense of its burthens, to be rid of all regulations. How it is practicable to keep the people duly armed without some organization, it is difficult to

see. There is certainly no small danger, that indifference may lead to disgust, and disgust to contempt; and thus gradually undermine all the protection intended by this clause of our national bill of rights.

Story's description of the Second Amendment points in two directions. Gun-rights proponents like the "palladium of liberty" phrase and its juxtaposition to the idea of a "check" on oppressive rulers. Yet the thrust of the passage lies in its references to the militia as a defense against oppression; taken as a whole, Story's description seems to require some sort of militia-related interpretation. It could be the militia-related individual-rights interpretation. It also could be the states' rights interpretation we'll examine in Chapter 2. For now, it's worth noting that Story seems a bit uncomfortable with any militia-related interpretation, given the actual state of the militia in the 1830s. We need a good militia to defend ourselves, Story seems to be saying, but we haven't got one, and the chances seem high that re-creating a good one is not "practicable" under current conditions.

The OLC memo adds another element to the Second Amendment narrative—the treatment of the right to keep and bear arms in early state constitutions. Here too the evidence points in two directions. The memo works through the texts of six state constitutional provisions. Like the good lawyers they are, the OLC's lawyers emphasize the provisions that are pretty clearly individual-rights provisions, and massage the others to make them fit the individual-rights view. In the end, though, the conclusions we can draw from those provisions is limited.

PENNSYLVANIA

Pennsylvania (and Vermont, which used the same language) provides the best individual-rights provisions. The Pennsylvania

Declaration of Rights (1776) asserted "[t]hat the people have a right to bear arms for the defence of themselves and the state; and as standing armies in the time of peace are dangerous to liberty, they ought not to be kept up." The state's 1790 constitution provided that "the right of the citizens to bear arms, in defence of themselves and the State, shall not be questioned." You can strain to read the separate references to defense of themselves and defense of the state to refer to a single enterprise—the defense of the people as organized into the state—but the natural reading is that the provision refers to a right of personal self-defense, which supports the individual-rights view. In addition, the constitutional provisions use the single term "bear arms" rather than the conjoined "keep and bear arms" with its military connotations.

VIRGINIA

The Virginia Declaration of Rights, also adopted in 1776, is more militia-oriented: "That a well regulated militia, composed of the body of the people, trained to arms, is the proper, natural, and safe defence of a free State; that standing armies, in time of peace, should be avoided, as dangerous to liberty." Here is the militia as the body of the people, but also a reference only to the defense of the state, with no overtones of self-defense at all. The language here, of course, is strikingly parallel to the Second Amendment's—no surprise, given that Virginian James Madison drafted the Second Amendment.

MASSACHUSETTS

Massachusetts's provision, adopted in 1780, is similar in structure to Virginia's: "The people have a right to keep and bear arms for the common defense. And, as, in time of peace, armies are dangerous to liberty, they ought not to be maintained without the consent of the legislature." Again: the reference to the common defense, not self-defense, and the juxtaposition of the right to bear arms next to worry about standing armies. Indeed, even the more individually oriented Pennsylvania provision placed the right to bear arms adjacent to concern about standing armies.

NORTH CAROLINA

North Carolina's provision (1776) uses Pennsylvania's phrase "defence of the State," but omits the "defense of themselves" and continues the pattern of associating the right with concern about standing armies: "That the people have a right to bear arms, for the defence of the State; and, as standing armies, in time of peace, are dangerous to liberty, they ought not to be kept up."

These provisions shed some light on a small detail in the Second Amendment's history. The information we have about the Senate's deliberations on the entire Bill of Rights are exceedingly thin. Basically, what we have are records of the votes the Senators cast on motions to adopt the proposed amendments, to alter them, and the like. On the Second Amendment, the Senate considered a motion to add four words to the proposal, so that it would refer to a right "to keep and bear arms for the common defence." The motion failed, which some gun-rights proponents say shows a choice for a provision that created an individual right. That, though, places too much weight on what was likely a preference for using fewer rather than more words to express a single idea.

What do gun-rights proponents make of these provisions? Obviously, they are fond of Pennsylvania's provision. The best the OLC's lawyers can do with the Virginia provision is to say that the "body of the people" phrase "is consistent with the right of individuals to have arms." They also argue that "[i]t would not have made sense, in the context of a state constitution, for a 'right' of 'the people' to protect only the prerogatives of the State." That's pretty clearly wrong: It's not the prerogative of the State to organize the militia that's in question, but its power to resist an oppressive national government. Having a right to arms so as to defend North Carolina against the new national government makes perfect sense.

So, what's the bottom line? Academics have written *a lot* about the Second Amendment and its history, and I can't pretend that my discussion here deals with every nuance of the arguments made by proponents of gun rights and those of gun control. The scholarship is full of broad claims, factoids, and counterpunching. A gun-control proponent cites a statement made in one of the conventions called to ratify the Constitution to support her position; some gun-rights proponent responds that, understood properly, that statement doesn't support the gun-control position; a third participant weighs in on the gun-control side to explain why the gun-rights response really isn't terribly effective—and on and on. The payoff for following the details of the argument rapidly diminishes. After all, lawyers know how to massage apparently adverse material so that it doesn't "really" count against the position they support. I've described the main lines of argument for the Standard Model without taking up *everything* that can be said in its favor and against it, omitting minor details or weak counterarguments.

The history we've reviewed, the quotations we've gone through, and the early state constitutional provisions we've analyzed provide substantial support for *some* individual rights interpretation, although I have to emphasize that "substantial support" is not "a slam-dunk, open-and-shut case." The best individual-rights interpretation connects the individual right to the operation of the citizen-militia: We each have the right to keep and bear arms so that we can participate in the militia—the body of the people—and thereby keep governments from becoming tyrants. The Second Amendment's preamble explains why the Constitution contains the right—to preserve "the security of a free state"—but doesn't impose conditions on exercising the right. Once each of us has the right to keep and bear arms, we can use the right however we want—but always preserving the possibility that we will use it to defend against government oppression.

In March 2007 the federal court of appeals for Washington, D.C., vindicated the OLC, striking down the District of Columbia's comprehensive prohibition on handgun possession. The District's law prohibited the city's residents from carrying handguns and even from moving a handgun from one room in their homes to another without a permit, and required that all lawfully owned firearms, such as shotguns, be kept unloaded and disassembled or disabled by a trigger lock. The court's opinion basically tracked the OLC memo—not surprising, because the memo laid out the strongest purely originalist argument for the individual-rights view of the Second Amendment. The opinion was written by Laurence Silberman, a long-term Republican activist and public servant, who had been deputy attorney general in the administration of Gerald Ford, ambassador to Yugoslavia under Ronald Reagan, an active supporter of Clarence Thomas during the controversy over Thomas's Supreme Court nomination, and co-chair of the Iraq Intelligence Commission appointed by President George W. Bush to investigate—some said whitewash—the intelligence leading up to the 2003 invasion of Iraq. Judge Silberman's opinion was joined by Judge Thomas Griffith, who had served as chief counsel to the United States Senate when it was controlled by Republicans between 1995 and 1999 and whose judicial nomination had been the subject of a minor flap when Democrats discovered that he had allowed his bar membership to lapse for a couple of years even though he continued to practice law. Judge Karen Henderson, another Republican appointee to the court, dissented.

The opinion's long-term impact cannot be known as I write. The entire court of appeals refused to consider the case. As Judge Henderson's vote indicates, the positions judges take on the Second Amendment's meaning do not straightforwardly track political backgrounds. The case seems headed for the Supreme Court, which—as we will see in the next chapter—has not considered a major Second Amendment case in more than sixty years. And finally, the District of Columbia gun law is probably the most restrictive in the nation. Concluding that the Second Amendment's protection of an individual right to keep and bear arms invalidates the city's law might have relatively little effect on other, more common and less absolutist gun regulations.

Remember reading in high school about Natty Bumppo, James Fenimore Cooper's "Deerslayer"? What do you think he used to kill the deers? Not a bow and arrow, but a rifle. His weapon wasn't just for hunting or self-defense, though. In one episode, Natty Bumppo shoots a deer out of season. Bumppo's adversary, Judge Marmaduke Temple, issues a questionable search warrant and deputizes some henchmen to arrest Bumppo. Arriving at Bumppo's hut, they are confronted with an armed man who resists their effort to search the hut: "The Leather-stocking now assumed a more threatening attitude; his rifle was in his hand." And, "when the fire-arms were introduced," the deputies retreated, offering to negotiate with Bumppo rather than to coerce him.

Cooper wrote in the 1820s, but the sturdy—and armed— frontiersman was already an icon in Americans' ways of understanding themselves. Weapons were important on the frontier not just to feed a man and his family. They defended him against marauders—which, as Bumppo knew, sometimes included government and its agents. *That* is the image on which the individual-rights interpretation of the Second Amendment draws.

Now we can return to our "gun license test" proposal. If the Second Amendment protects an individual right, it would seem obvious that you can't be required to pass a test before you acquire a gun. The government can make you pass a test before you drive a car, because nothing in the Constitution gives you a right to drive. But it can't require you to pass a test before you publish a newspaper or start your own blog, because you do have a constitutional right, under the First Amendment, to free speech. Nor can the government require you to pass a civics test before you serve on a jury, because you have a constitutional right to serve (or more precisely, a right not to be excluded for reasons unrelated to the *parties'* judgment about your qualifications). And it can't require you to pass a test before you get a gun, for exactly the same reason.

CHAPTER TWO

The Standard Model
and Developments Since 1791

TODAY'S WORLD IS very different from the one Americans lived in when they adopted the Second Amendment. It's not realistic these days to think of an armed citizenry defending us against an oppressive government. That doesn't mean, though, that we have to replace every possible individual-rights interpretation with something else. A Second Amendment that protected our right to keep and bear arms so that we can defend ourselves against criminals, for example, wouldn't be ruled out by modern developments. And, as we'll see, there's a way of connecting that kind of Second Amendment right to the amendment's reference to the militia. To see how, we have to identify changes in our society that make obsolete the idea of protecting the right to keep and bear arms as part of the citizen-militia.

THE DISAPPEARANCE OF CIVIC REPUBLICANISM

Law professor David Williams argues, for example, that the founding generation really did experience the body of the people acting collectively without organization by the government. Towns and even cities were small, and people knew who their neighbors were. There was, according to Williams, a real community that could be mobilized to resist oppression. That community, he says, has now disappeared. Cities and suburbs are simply places where large numbers of people live, anonymous to each other. "The people" no longer can act as a united body resisting an oppressive government. Gun owners are not the body of the people, but only a segment of the society. As Williams once put it, these developments have made the militia-related individual-rights interpretation of the Second Amendment "meaningless" and "outdated." Proponents of a related interpretation write that "the term 'militia' in anything approaching its original sense has...simply outlived its application. While not gone from the constitutional landscape, it is an empty shell, devoid of effect in the real world of today."

Gun-rights proponents respond, "So what?" Consider another imaginary constitutional provision with an explanatory preamble: "Bows and arrows being useful to protect the people against woolly mammoths, the right of the people to keep and bear bows and arrows shall not be infringed." Let's assume that bows and arrows really were useful against woolly mammoths when this constitutional provision was adopted. Does the right to keep and bear bows and arrows disappear when woolly mammoths do? Maybe so, but it's hardly obvious that it would. And, even more, we ought to reject an interpretation of *any* constitutional provision that makes it meaningless—at least as long as some other interpretation is available. We have a way to get rid of constitutional provisions that have become outdated; it's called "repealing them," not "interpreting them out of existence."

TECHNOLOGICAL CHANGE

A different kind of obsolescence is more troubling to the citizen-militia view. When the Second Amendment was adopted, guns and rifles might have been thought sufficient to keep a government bent on tyranny at bay. The body of the people armed with guns and rifles could be intimidating enough to keep the government in line, or to successfully resist oppression. Today that's simply not true. The government has armored personnel carriers and nuclear weapons. Handguns and rifles can't possibly be enough to resist the armed forces of today's governments.

Gun-rights proponents divide over the implications of technological change. Some rely on the British background of the Second Amendment and accept that "dangerous or unusual arms" can be prohibited. One prominent gun-rights advocate concludes that governments can ban private ownership of flamethrowers, armor-piercing bullets, and even high-powered rifles that can go through walls and injure innocent by-standers. Another, though, relies on the meaning of "bear" to argue that the Second Amendment would be violated if the government banned the possession of weapons that could be carried outside the home—including switchblade knives and any firearms that could be used against an attacker. Fortunately, he does exclude "artillery pieces, tanks, [and] nuclear devices," and has an exception as well for "grenades, bombs, bazookas, and other devices which, while capable of being carried by hand, have never been commonly possessed for self-defense."

Of course, shoulder-carried Stinger missiles haven't been commonly possessed for self-defense because they are technological innovations—and so really do exemplify the challenge gun-control proponents throw up against gun-rights advocates. The ad hoc exceptions seem designed to avoid the charge of fanaticism rather than to explain the logic of the gun-rights position. It should be clear why advocates of the citizen-militia interpretation of the Second Amendment can't respond to incredulity at the possibility that the Amendment protects the right to keep and bear bazookas by saying that restricting *that* right is part of the "regulation" referred to in the amendment's preamble: Such a regulation deprives the amendment of its point, which is to give the body of the people the means to resist an oppressive government by armed force.

Perhaps the modern technology of oppression has made the Second Amendment obsolete were it taken to protect only the right to keep and bear guns and rifles, and ridiculous were it taken to protect the right to keep and bear bazookas. As a matter of pure legal analysis, we *could* have ridiculous constitutional provisions: "Of course it's ridiculous, but it's in the Constitution, and that's enough to force us to follow it." But once lots of people come to think that a constitutional provision is ridiculous, the provision won't limit what governments do. I suspect that would be true if we could make sense of the Second Amendment only by interpreting it to protect the right to keep and bear bazookas.

There's one escape hatch, which some gun-rights proponents use. They concede that the Second Amendment doesn't give us a right to own bazookas but argue that successful guerilla movements show that people whose weaponry is far inferior to that of their opponents can nonetheless succeed. So, they suggest, people armed only with handguns and rifles could do a lot to slow down an oppressive government armed with tanks and machine guns. The right to keep and bear small arms, then, hasn't become obsolescent.

There's another way out, though. We can supplement the citizen-militia interpretation in a way that makes sense, today, of a Second Amendment right to keep and bear handguns. Gun-rights proponents have increasingly focused on the use of guns for self-defense against criminal depredations. Fitting a concern for self-defense into the originalist framework has to be done with some care, but once it's done, the individual-rights interpretation retains its force. As we've seen, when the Second Amendment was adopted, there were two ways of articulating the right to keep and bear arms. One simply invoked the citizen-militia right. The Massachusetts Constitution of 1780 said, "The people have a right to keep and to bear arms for the common defence." The other added to that right an explicit reference to a right of self-defense. The Pennsylvania Constitution of 1790, for example, said, "The right of the citizens to bear arms in defence of [a] themselves and [b] the State shall not be questioned." The Second Amendment chose the first rather than the second formulation.

Why doesn't that choice exclude self-defense from the explanation for why we have the Second Amendment? Maybe the self-defense argument was sufficiently widespread that the two formulations weren't understood to be significantly different: For many in the founding era, the relation between self-defense and the right to keep and bear arms was so obvious that it literally went without saying—as in the Second Amendment.

There's another and I think better response available to gun-rights proponents. The citizen-militia view focuses on one kind of government failure—tyranny and oppression—and relies on the armed body of the people to protect us against that kind of failure. But governments can fail in other ways. We strike a deal when we form a government: We will give up some of our "natural" rights in exchange for the benefits we get—especially, protection against attackers—from government. Sometimes, though, the government doesn't keep its side of the deal. It fails to provide us with the basic good of individual security, the very purpose for which we created the government in the first place. A government that permits widespread criminality to persist is as much a failure as a government that throws its opponents in jail. A right to keep and bear arms for self-defense responds to *that* kind of government failure.

One minor objection: Who gets to decide that the government has failed to provide adequate security against criminals? There's a difference between the "oppressive government" and "failure to provide security" situations. The militia is a group of people, and you can't effectively resist the government on your own. So there's an inherent check on your judgment that the government has become oppressive: You have to get other people to agree with you. It's not clear that there's a similar check on judgments that the government has failed to provide adequate security. Each person who suffers an attack might conclude that the very fact of attack demonstrates government failure. This objection doesn't have much bite, though, when the question is whether the possibility of government failure *explains* why we have a right to keep and bear arms (and not whether that possibility is a condition for having the right). Suppose a homeowner uses those arms in self-defense and claims to be justified because the government failed to protect us. Judges and juries can evaluate that justification on a case-by-case basis, and the fact that they decide that the homeowner wasn't justified under the circumstances doesn't cast any doubt on the proposition that we have a right to keep and bear arms for purposes of self-defense when the government fails to keep its side of the bargain.

In the end, we might have a right to keep and bear handguns for self-defense even if we don't have any right to keep and bear the kinds of weapons that would be needed today to resist an oppressive government.

So far I've argued that the Second Amendment as originally understood probably protected some sort of individual right associated with the militia as the entire body of the people but might today be taken to protect an individual right because of our need for self-defense. Both versions are originalist because they pay attention to the problem, which those who adopted the Amendment cared about, of governments that fail to do what they should.

There's another, though related, possibility: The right is one that we each hold (so it's an individual right), because we are *citizens* in a representative democracy. Keeping and bearing arms is a duty *and* a right, just as service on juries is.

To see how the Second Amendment might be a citizen's right associated with the militia, the place to begin is with the militia as it operated in America before and during the Revolution. Citizen-soldiers turned out to be terrible soldiers. They couldn't be relied on to show up and fight, and when they did, they couldn't be counted on to use their weapons accurately. In a dyspeptic letter reflecting on his experience leading a militia during the French and Indian Wars of the 1750s, George Washington wrote,

Militia, you will find, Sir, will never answer your expectation, no dependence is to be placed upon them; They are obstinate and perverse, they are often egged on by the Officers, who lead them to acts of disobedience, and, when they are ordered to certain posts for the security of stores, or the protection of the Inhabitants, will, on a sudden, resolve to leave *them*, and the united vigilance of their officers can not prevent them.

Washington's views about citizen-soldiers didn't change, and as we've seen he was one of the strongest voices for establishing a professional, standing army for the United States.

The perceived inadequacies of the citizen militia are important in the Second Amendment's development, according to the citizen-right view. To those who feared standing armies, the trick was to *create* (or, as they might have put it, re-create) a body of the

[35]

people who *could* be the kind of militia that they thought necessary. The Second Amendment was their vehicle for doing so. The Amendment was understood to reflect the idea that citizens had a *duty* to participate in the militia. We can see this from several angles.

• James Madison's draft of what became the Second Amendment looks a lot like the final version, with one major exception. Madison proposed this: "The right of the people to keep and bear arms shall not be infringed; a well armed and well regulated militia being the best security of a free country: but no person religiously scrupulous of bearing arms shall be compelled to render military service in person." The final clause, on religious exemptions, was soon dropped. The puzzle is, What was it doing there in the first place? Saul Cornell, who has developed the citizen-right view most extensively, answers that Madison assumed that militia service was a citizen's duty. Everyone should take part in the militia, and the government could do what was necessary to ensure that participation. The religious exemption reflected principles of religious freedom, counseling against coercing people to do things that violated their religious beliefs.

• The citizen-oriented interpretation is bolstered by the amendment's reference to a "well regulated" militia. Just as citizens had a duty to participate in the militia, governments had a duty to train the citizen-soldiers and to provide them with arms when they could not do so on their own. "Well regulated" describes this public duty.

• Finally, right after the Second Amendment came into effect, Congress passed the Militia Act of 1792. The act required states to enroll—that is, list as members of the militia—"each and every able-bodied white male citizen" between the ages of eighteen and forty-five, with exceptions for a bunch of federal officials ranging from the vice president down to customs-house officers, postal "stage drivers," and ferrymen. This was Congress's effort to identify the militia with the body of the people. And then came the citizens' duties:

> [E]very citizen, so enrolled and notified, shall, within six months thereafter, provide himself with a good musket or firelock, a sufficient bayonet and belt, two spare flints, and a knapsack, a pouch, with a box therein, to contain not less than twenty four cartridges, suited to the bore of his musket or firelock, each cartridge to contain a proper quantity of power and ball; or with a good rifle, knapsack, shot-pouch, and power-horn, twenty balls suited to the bore of his rifle, and a quarter of a pound of powder; and shall appear so armed, accoutred and provided, when called out to exercise or into service, except, that when called out on company days to exercise only, he may appear without a knapsack.... [T]he commissioned Officers shall severally be armed with a sword or hanger, and espontoon; and ... from and after five years from the passing of this Act, all muskets from arming the militia as is herein required, shall be of bores sufficient for balls of the eighteenth part of a pound.

The idea of duty is on the surface here. And, as the OLC memo says, the Militia Act—and the concept of "good regulation"—presupposes that most militia members, which is to say most members of the body of the people, will and certainly should have weapons adequate for their militia participation.

What are the implications of the citizen-oriented interpretation today? Obsolescence, the decay of civic participation generally, may suggest that today's citizens don't have an individual right to keep and bear arms. But were civic participation to rise, or were governments to take up once again their duty to produce an alert citizenry, perhaps an individual right to keep and bear arms might once again spring up. Yet this approach reminds us of a number of citizen duties—to sit on juries, to participate in the militia, to have weapons adequate for that participation—which seem to be pretty reasonably lodged in individuals. I'm inclined to think that it's easier to see this interpretation as treating the Second Amendment to create what I would call, awkwardly, a citizen-oriented individual right to keep and bear arms. The amendment's reference to the militia reminds us of our civic duties, but it doesn't limit the scope of the individual right. This interpretation is one that gun-rights proponents should find appealing.

What then of the proposal that gun-owners have to pass a test on their knowledge of firearms and on their ability to use them safely? Perhaps a good citizen would want to demonstrate civic responsibility by taking and passing a test. But think about jury service: People called to be part of the jury pool in Washington, D.C., are shown a short movie about their responsibilities as jurors; they are not tested—because jury service is their right. So too with taking a licensing test to own a gun. The government can do a lot to encourage citizens to use guns responsibly, but it cannot, on the view developed in this chapter, keep them from owning guns without demonstrating civic responsibility.

The Second Amendment is in the *United States* Constitution. Of course states have their own constitutions, and many of them have parallels to the Second Amendment. These provisions limit the power of state and local governments to regulate guns. Typically, though, the state equivalents of the Second Amendment appear to allow more gun control than gun-rights advocates think appropriate. Does the Second Amendment itself limit the degree to which states and cities can regulate guns?

In *Barron v. Mayor and City Council of Baltimore* (1833), the Supreme Court held that the Bill of Rights imposed limits on the national government, not on state or local governments. The case involved John Barron's wharf in Baltimore harbor. As the city grew, the harbor got polluted and shallower, making it harder for Barron to make money because he couldn't accommodate as many ships at the wharf. He sued the city, claiming that its failure to clean up the harbor violated the Fifth Amendment's takings clause, which says, "nor shall private property be taken without just compensation." His point was that the Fifth Amendment limited *every* government in the United States, not just the national government. Compare the Fifth Amendment and its passive voice—or the Second Amendment's reference to "the right of the people"—with the First Amendment, whose first word is "Congress." Barron's lawyers said that the comparison shows that the Bill of Rights itself distinguishes between limits placed only on the national government, like the First Amendment, and limits placed on all governments, such as the Fifth Amendment—and the Second. Chief Justice John Marshall and the Supreme Court rejected Barron's argument, not because the city's inaction wasn't a "taking" but because the Bill of Rights limited only the national government. The rights in the Bill of Rights "are limitations of power granted in the instrument itself, not of distinct governments framed by different persons and for different purposes." Chief Justice Marshall wrote, "it is universally understood, it is a part of the history of the day" that the Bill of Rights was an effort to ensure that the new national government would not violate the rights identified there, and that when it was adopted people weren't worrying about oppression by state governments: "These amendments demanded security against the apprehended encroachments of the General Government—not against those of the local governments."

The Second Amendment doesn't limit state and local governments, then. But that's not the end of the constitutional story. After the Civil War ended, Congress proposed and the states ratified the Fourteenth Amendment, which *does* limit state power: "No State shall make or enforce any law which shall abridge the privileges or immunities of citizens of the United States." To understand the Privileges or Immunities Clause, we have to go back before the Civil War. The most radical opponents of slavery developed constitutional arguments that slavery was unconstitutional under the original Constitution and the Bill of Rights. Of course, slavery was established by state law, so these theorists had to explain why the Bill of Rights limited state power. They did so in part by saying that the Barron decision was wrong.

A second strand in pre–Civil War abolitionist theorizing involved a provision in the original Constitution saying that "the Citizens of each State shall be entitled to all Privileges and Immunities of Citizens in the several States." The most prominent court interpretation of this provision came in a decision written by Justice Bushrod Washington (George Washington's favorite nephew) in 1823. What rights did the original Privileges and Immunities Clause protect? Justice Washington, writing not for the Supreme Court but for one of the lower federal courts, listed some, and then gave a general description: "those privileges and immunities which are, in their nature, fundamental; which belong, of right, to the citizens of all free governments." Abolitionist constitutional theorists argued that freedom itself was a fundamental "privilege and immunity." So for them, it had to be true that free blacks who traveled to South Carolina had the right to walk freely on Charleston's streets, notwithstanding a South

Carolina law purporting to bar black seaman from entering the city. And pushing the argument further, abolitionist theorists argued that slavery itself violated the Privileges and Immunities Clause.

These abolitionist constitutional theorists didn't prevail before the Civil War, of course. But their thinking fed into that of the men who drafted and ratified the Fourteenth Amendment. So did the experience of African Americans and their "carpetbagger" supporters in the South immediately after the Civil War. The South had lost the military conflict, but many southern whites were recalcitrant. The first governments they created after the Civil War ended enacted what were known as the Black Codes. These codes attempted to keep African Americans under controls almost as tight as they had faced as slaves. They restricted the ability of African Americans to move freely. And importantly, they restricted the right of African American free persons to own guns.

These restrictions mattered a lot, because some southern whites engaged in a campaign of terror against African Americans. Deprived of weapons, the free black population was vulnerable to attacks from the Ku Klux Klan. As we'll see in a moment, shortly after the Bill of Rights was adopted, political leaders began to worry a lot about the possibility that the self-organized citizens' militia might become the vehicle for anarchic resistance to valid laws. Republican politicians saw in the Ku Klux Klan the very epitome of such a "militia." In response, Congress displaced the white-dominated state governments with military rule. The South's military governors repealed the Black Codes and made gun possession by free blacks legal. With their newly protected rights in hand, southern blacks renewed the militia tradition and organized themselves—both within and outside the framework created by the state-organized militia—for self-defense against the Klan and other terrorists. One self-organized citizen militia might then act, along with the national government, against another such militia. Supporters of African American rights in Congress, drafting the Fourteenth Amendment, came to see weapons possession as one of the privileges and immunities free citizens had to have.

Senator Jacob Howard chaired the committee charged with overseeing the military governments in the South. When he presented the draft of the Fourteenth Amendment to the Senate, he said that the Privileges or Immunities Clause covered at least "the personal rights guarantied and secured by the first eight Amendments to the Constitution; such as the freedom of speech... [and] the right to keep and to bear arms." Representative John Bingham, the Amendment's principal drafter, repeatedly asserted that the amendment was designed to overturn the Barron decision that the Bill of Rights limited only the national government and make the Bill of Rights—without qualification—applicable as a limit on state and local governments as well. In constitutional parlance, this is described as the "incorporation" of the Second Amendment into the Fourteenth.

The last brick in the argument for treating the Second Amendment, incorporated into the Fourteenth Amendment, as an "individual rights" limitation on state and local governments comes from changes in the way Americans understood the right to keep and bear arms. I've argued that the citizen-militia or citizen-related interpretations of the individual right to keep and bear arms were somewhat stronger than the pure individual rights interpretation—in the 1790s. But things changed between 1800 and 1860. The idea of the militia as the body of the people became less compelling as Americans got used to democratic government. But the idea that people should have an individual right to keep and bear arms for purposes of self-defense, hunting, and anything else they wanted to use weapons for—that is, the pure individual rights view—got increasing support in state law. Regulations of that individual right were of course permitted, but the right itself came more and more to be understood as a pure individual right. When the Fourteenth Amendment barred state and local governments from making laws that abridge "privileges or immunities," it limited the power of those governments to regulate the individual right to keep and bear arms.

The constitutional history of the application of the Bill of Rights to the states is long and complex. The short version is this: Fairly soon after the Fourteenth Amendment was adopted the Supreme Court held that it did *not* make Bill of Rights protections applicable to state governments. Over the next decades, the Court started to say that states *were* barred from violating fundamental rights—but explicitly said that not every guarantee in the Bill of Rights was fundamental. Then, in the 1920s and 1930s, the Court, while continuing to say that specific Bill of Rights provisions were not incorporated into the Fourteenth Amendment, began to apply the "fundamental rights" test in a few cases where it certainly looked as if it was actually invoking one or another of the rights listed in the Bill of Rights. Supreme Court justices Felix Frankfurter and Hugo Black engaged in a two-decade battle over whether the Fourteenth Amendment incorporated *all* of the listed rights (and no others), which was Black's position, or whether it incorporated *none* of them (but did require fundamental fairness of the states), which was Frankfurter's.

The breakthrough came after Frankfurter retired because of illness. Instead of incorporating the Bill of Rights in a single decision, the Warren Court engaged in a process that came to be called *selective* incorporation. In case after case, the Warren Court said that the protections of first one amendment, then another, were so important that they were indeed components of the fundamental fairness that the Fourteenth Amendment required of states. By the 1970s, *every* right set out in the Bill of Rights had been selectively incorporated—except for three: the right to have serious criminal charges started by a grand jury's decision (in the Fifth Amendment), the right to a jury trial in civil cases where the stakes are more than $20 (in the Seventh Amendment), and the Second Amendment right to keep and bear arms.

Surely the right to keep and bear arms is at least as important as other rights that have been selectively incorporated, and certainly it isn't the kind of triviality that the Seventh Amendment's civil jury right is. Intellectual honesty requires that the courts take the next step and decide that the Fourteenth Amendment guarantees the right to keep and bear arms against state regulations just as the Second Amendment does against regulations by the national government.

The Fourteenth Amendment matters in another way. Some critics of originalist approaches to constitutional interpretation wonder why we should care about what the restricted electorate of the founding era—white and male—thought about the Constitution's meaning. The Second Amendment might be a good target for such criticism. The body of the people that constituted the militia was, after all, white and male (and able-bodied). The Second Amendment wouldn't carry much moral weight today were the only people with a right to keep and bear arms to be the members of the body of the people as of 1791.

The Fourteenth Amendment shows that we don't have to interpret the Second Amendment that narrowly. Rather, the body of the people consists of all those who are, at any time, treated as full citizens. In 1791 that included whites and males—and excluded those who had been loyal to England during the Revolution, as well as women and slaves. Today every member of the political community has an individual right to keep and bear arms. We can argue about how to treat denial of gun rights to those convicted of serious crimes: Maybe the denial is a reasonable regulation, maybe it follows from the proposition that those criminals aren't full members of the political community. But the central cases—women and African Americans—are easy.

The individual-rights view of the Second Amendment is that each of us has a right to keep and bear arms for whatever reasons we want. We don't have to use the weapons for militia-related purposes. Disconnecting the Amendment's preamble—again, "a well regulated Militia, being necessary to the security of a free State"—from the right it creates provides a sensible response to nervous observations about an individual right to resist an oppressive government by armed force. Those concerns are captured by thinking about the Ku Klux Klan's depredations in the post–Civil War South, and how they might recur today: Timothy McVeigh appears to have thought that the United States government had become oppressive, and the various self-identified citizen "militias" in places like Michigan and Idaho make the same claim. It can't be that McVeigh and those "militias" have a right protected by the Second Amendment to offer armed resistance to the government simply because the Second Amendment is explained as ensuring that an oppressive government can be met with armed resistance.

And on the individual-rights view, they don't. What they have is an individual right to keep and bear arms. They can be punished for abusing that right. If prosecutors think that the militias have abused their rights, for example, by offering armed resistance to governments that the militias think are oppressive, they can haul the militia's members before a jury of their co-citizens, who will acquit them if they agree that the government had become oppressive, or convict them if they disagree. The militia-*related* individual-rights view doesn't have to worry about figuring out who gets to lead the unorganized citizen-militia, or who gets to decide when a government has become oppressive. The Second Amendment's preamble doesn't limit the right to keep and bear arms to circumstances of oppression; all it does is explain why the amendment's adopters thought it important to give individuals the right to keep and bear arms. The Second Amendment makes it unconstitutional for governments to confiscate ordinary weapons and might place some other limits on what governments can treat as abuses of the right to keep and bear arms. It does not establish a right to anarchy.

CHAPTER THREE

. . .

The Traditional Interpretation

GUN-CONTROL PROPONENTS had a predictable reaction to the conclusion by the Department of Justice that the Second Amendment protected an individual right. Sarah Brady, wife of Ronald Reagan's press secretary James Brady, became a gun-control activist after her husband suffered severe brain damage in John Hinckley's attempted assassination of President Reagan. She became chair of the Campaign to Prevent Gun Violence, an offshoot of a long-standing gun-control lobbying group, in 1991. When the Department of Justice memorandum was published, she attacked it as a "discredited interpretation held by the gun lobby." She continued, John Ashcroft's "position is also dangerous, as it would only make defending reasonable gun laws—laws that Americans overwhelmingly support—more difficult." Earlier Garry Wills had written of "the linguistic tricks of the Standard Model which wrench terms from context and impose fanciful meanings on them."

What is the real meaning of the Second Amendment? We saw some hints of it in the discussion of the Department of Justice's "individual rights" view. Gun-control proponents offer instead something usually called the "collective rights" view, although it's probably better described as a "states' rights" view. The Second Amendment protects the right of states to organize their own militias—roughly, the state-organized National Guard we have today. On this interpretation, the licensing-test proposal poses no constitutional problems whatever. Owning a gun is indeed just like driving a car—not a personal right protected by the Constitution, but a privilege that legislatures can regulate as much as we the voters are willing to tolerate.

There are hints of the "collective rights" interpretation in the debates over adopting the Constitution and the Second Amendment, although there those hints are distinctly subordinate to the more robust discussions of the right of every citizen to own weapons for purposes of dealing with a tyrannical or inept government. The collective-rights view came into its own, though, over the course of the nineteenth and twentieth centuries.

The collective-rights view begins, of course, with the Constitution's text. Not the text of the Second Amendment, but that of the original, unamended Constitution. The original Constitution refers to militias several times, and each time the obvious reference is to state-organized military forces.

As we saw in Chapter 1, the founding generation was quite nervous about the creation of a national standing army. Militias were to serve as a counterweight to the national government's armed force. States would organize "select" militias, drawn from the overall white male citizenry, for that purpose. But, the founders believed, these select militias could also be a partial substitute for a standing army. So they gave the national government the power to call the state militias into national service "to execute the Laws of the Union, suppress Insurrections and repel Invasions." *These* constitutional references clearly deal with state-organized military forces. The term *militia* in the Second Amendment refers to the same entity—the state-organized select militia—that the term referred to in the original, unamended Constitution. According to the collective-rights view, the Second Amendment responded to concern that the reservation of state power to appoint officers and train the militia wasn't enough to prevent the national government from totally eliminating the state-organized militias. As George Mason put it in articulating his objections to the original Constitution: "The militia may here be destroyed ... by rendering them useless—by disarming them. Under various pretexts, Congress may neglect to provide for arming and disciplining the militia" and substitute a standing army. The Second Amendment is a states' rights provision that ensures that the national government can't disarm state-organized militias. It has no bearing whatever on regulation—including prohibition—of gun ownership by people who aren't members of the state-organized militias.

The original version of the Second Amendment, with its provision for conscientious objectors, supports the collective-rights interpretation. A provision guaranteeing individuals the right to keep and bear arms wouldn't have to contain an exemption for such objectors because they would simply choose not to own weapons. On the collective-rights view, the exemption makes sense only if the provision as a whole referred to state-organized military forces. The religious exemption was dropped because of concern that religious exemptions would interfere with the functioning of the armed forces, not to change the proposal's meaning.

You can find scattered expressions during the run-up to the Second Amendment's adoption consistent with this states' rights interpretation of the Second Amendment, but you have to work pretty hard to elevate them into a position of primary importance. More significant were changes in thinking and experience in the new republic's first two decades.

The new Constitution changed the way people were governed in ways that reduced many of the concerns they had about the British monarchy. Obviously, the national government was the creature of the American people acting in a representative democracy. In several of the *Federalist Papers* James Madison offered the classic defense of the proposition that the new national government posed no serious threat to the liberties of Americans: The national government's powers were limited by listing them in the Constitution; the system known variously as separation of powers or checks and balances made it extremely difficult for the national government to enact and enforce oppressive laws; and— in a development that was foreshadowed early and confirmed in 1803—the courts were available to strike down laws that violated specific constitutional guarantees The new national government, then, posed a much smaller risk of the kinds of tyranny that might require the forceful resistance that the general militia—an armed citizenry—could provide. All the quotations from the Declaration of Rights, Blackstone, and other pre-constitutional sources don't add up to much because they were written in a context where representative democracy either didn't really exist or hadn't taken firm hold.

Armed resistance to national legislation in a democratic republic presented an old problem in a new guise. As we saw in Chapter 2, the problem was distinguishing between justified resistance to tyranny and anarchy or mob rule. Citizens sitting on juries *might* be able to draw the distinction when a group sets itself up as a citizen-militia, thereby discouraging anarchic rebellion. The collective-rights interpretation attacks the problem more directly, by denying that individuals have any rights under the Second Amendment, when they act outside the state organized militia. The collective-rights interpretation guarantees law and order; the individual-rights one does not.

Two episodes, one just before the Constitution was adopted and one in the 1790s, framed the concern. Farmers in western Massachusetts experienced great financial stress in 1786. They were being taxed—in their view, too heavily—to pay the debts the state had incurred during the Revolutionary War. And they were cash-poor, which meant that they were forced to sell their farms to pay the taxes. Daniel Shays was a war veteran who assembled a band of rebels, amounting by some estimates to over 9,000 men over the several months of rebellion. They called themselves "Regulators" and understood themselves to be a militia in the classical sense. These militias marched into several towns in western Massachusetts and forced courthouses to close, stopping the forced farm sales. A "militia" of about 2,500 men attacked the state arsenal at Springfield, and smaller groups engaged in hit-and-run guerilla attacks on public buildings, lawyers, and politicians. The state government was unable to maintain order, but eventually another militia organized by merchants confronted and defeated the Shaysites by June 1787. Shays's Rebellion demonstrated to the Constitution's framers the need for a more powerful national government and suggested to some that the militia tradition needed to be modified in the nation's new circumstances. The Second Amendment's reference to a "well regulated militia" indicates the founders' discomfort at the possibility that the whole body of the people—a mob—would claim the authority of a militia.

The Whiskey Rebellion of 1794 was another protest against taxes, this time imposed by the national government to pay off the Revolutionary War debts that the government had taken over from the states. Whiskey producers in western Pennsylvania offered armed resistance to tax collectors, again acting in what they saw as the militia tradition. Several hundred men burned the home of the regional tax collector. President George Washington called out the state-organized militias of Pennsylvania, supplemented by forces from Maryland, Virginia, and New Jersey. Washington attempted to negotiate a peaceful settlement through a vote in western Pennsylvania but was unhappy with the result. He deployed the militias he had assembled, using them as the military occupiers of the region. This was enough to defeat the rebels.

The militia tradition was proving troublesome in the new republic. Could the Second Amendment be interpreted to accommodate concern about militias as undemocratic mobs rather than as the upright citizenry defending liberty against tyranny? The answer is, Of course. We have to interpret the Second Amendment in light of the political theory that was its background. That background—representative democracy—is one in which the people have a substantially greater say in governing themselves than the colonists (or even ordinary Englishmen) did when the militia tradition developed. The ability to elect your own representatives provides a pretty good substitute for most of what the militia tradition sought to accomplish—control by the people of those who exercised power in their name. Couple that with the difficulty of distinguishing, in a democratic society, between upright citizen militias and disorderly mobs, and the background political theory counsels against an individual-rights interpretation of the Second Amendment. And couple *that* with the social costs of allowing anyone to designate himself as a member of a militia resisting government tyranny, and we have a strong argument against the Standard Model—at least if there's a decent alternative interpretation available.

What about the use of guns for self-defense? Again, the background political theory matters. The self-defense interpretation makes sense when the government doesn't have organized police forces. What else but self-defense is there to protect yourself against criminals? The situation changes once governments create real police forces. Those forces provide a great deal of defense against criminal depredations. Of course the defense is imperfect, and you do have a right to defend yourself under some circumstances. But the reason is *not*, as the self-defense theory of the Second Amendment would have it, simply because the government hasn't done so. The situation is just like the one that arises when a self-styled militia mobilizes against what its members say is tyranny—and when the rest of us think that they are just a mob. That is, the self-defense theory is transformed once governments actually try reasonably hard to provide protection against criminals. After that, it's not really up to individuals to say that the fact of a criminal assault demonstrates the kind of government failure that justifies the individual right to bear arms under the self-defense theory.

The states' rights theory can be bolstered by paying attention to the National Guard as the successor to the citizen-militia. The past two centuries have seen a transformation of the militia into the National Guard. The National Guard has taken over the functions served in the founding era by the *un*organized militia, not simply those of the state-organized militias. The reasons for that change should inform our interpretation of the Second Amendment. Experience with the citizen-militia during the Revolutionary War began a process of disenchantment. Citizen-soldiers were adequate for guerilla warfare but not for sustained engagements with professional armies. Efforts to train citizens to use arms well were unsuccessful. People simply didn't show up for the militia "musters," as they were called. Something had to be done if militias were to be either a substitute for or a complement to a standing army.

What was done was to enhance the training and organization of the state-organized select militias. The process eventually produced the National Guard we have today. Better trained than the state-organized militias of the 1790s, and certainly better trained than most ordinary citizens today (better even than many ardent gun enthusiasts), the National Guard does what the citizen-militia was supposed to do. This eliminates the need for an individual right to keep and bear arms.

Of course, gun-rights proponents disagree. The argument focuses on only one of the militia's roles, overlooking the fact that state-organized militias could *never* be the right place to locate the citizen-militia individual right because state governments no less than the national one could become oppressive in ways that citizen-soldiers should resist.

The states' rights theory offers an alternative interpretation of the Second Amendment that would eliminate the need to distinguish between citizen-militias and mobs, and between government failures and an excessive individual response to a criminal's attack. But constitutional ideas change slowly, and once again we can only see glimpses of the states' rights theory before it came into its own in the late nineteenth century.

One hint came in the first Supreme Court opinion mentioning the Second Amendment. *Houston v. Moore* was a procedurally complex case decided in 1820. Houston was a private in the Pennsylvania militia, which had been ordered into national service by the state's governor on request of President James Madison. Houston didn't show up for service, was court-martialed, and fined. A state marshal seized some of Houston's property, and he sued the marshal in state court for trespassing on his land. The marshal relied on a *state* statute saying that militia members who were court-martialed had to pay the fines set out in a *federal* statute. Houston responded that the state statute was unconstitutional. The Supreme Court disagreed and upheld the seizure of Houston's property.

Justice Joseph Story, who as we saw in Chapter 1 described the right to keep and bear arms as "the palladium of the liberties of a republic," dissented. For him, Congress's power to prescribe regulations for the militia once called into national service excluded any state power under the circumstances. The general problem of how national power related to state power was important at the time, and Justice Story deployed his general views on its solution: Once Congress did *anything* to regulate state-organized militias, states lost all power—including the power to "organize, arm, and discipline" their militias. On the flip side, if Congress hadn't acted, Justice Story wrote, the state probably could "organize, arm, and discipline its own militia." And here he referred to the Second Amendment (which, oddly, he called the "fifth amendment"—maybe he had Blackstone's fifth auxiliary right on his brain). It might not "have any important bearing" on the case, but if it did, Justice Story wrote, "it confirms and illustrates, rather than impugns" his reasoning. This is very indirect, but it at least hints at the possibility that the Second Amendment was mostly about state-organized militias.

Around the time the Houston case was decided, what Saul Cornell calls "America's first gun control movement" provided another occasion for rethinking what the right to keep and bear arms protected. That movement, like more recent ones, was provoked by the perception that violence had gotten out of hand. Instead of walking away from arguments, people were pulling out knives and guns. Starting in the 1810s and persisting through the years before the Civil War, state legislatures responded by enacting laws prohibiting the carrying of concealed weapons.

Defendants responded by invoking state constitutional guarantees of the right to keep and bear arms.

Tennessee's Supreme Court was the first to consider a law against carrying concealed weapons. In a decision gun-rights proponents sometimes cite, it found the prohibition to violate the state's constitutional guarantees. The state legislature excoriated the decision, and the state's next constitution repudiated the result by specifically authorizing legislation against concealed weapons. After that first decision, the trend ran against defendants and their view of the right to keep and bear arms. In *Aymette v. State* (1840), the Tennessee Supreme Court upheld a law against Bowie knives. The court said that the right to keep and bear arms rested on the need for some way for the people to unite "for their common defense to vindicate their rights." That need was satisfied by the militia, and it followed, the court said, that the right to keep and bear arms protected the possession *only* of weapons that might be used by the militia. Notably, the court expressly excluded hunting rifles as well as concealed pistols from the right's coverage. Several things stand out in this opinion. First, the right was still militia-connected. Second, the relevant militia was not the state-organized militia but the armed citizenry generally. But third, the right's connection to an individual right—to hunt, or to defend oneself against a purely individual attack—was substantially weakened. The court's decision meant that the right to keep and bear arms protected only a collective right. Gun-rights proponents correctly observe that the collective was the white male population as a whole. But again, the possibility of an interpretation of the right more compatible with the views of gun-control proponents had increased.

The same can be said about a second notable ante bellum opinion, this one by the Arkansas Supreme Court in upholding the constitutionality of a state statute prohibiting carrying concealed weapons. Summing up an extended discourse on the political theory explaining the relation between organized government and natural rights, Chief Justice Daniel Ringo asked "for . . . what object the right to keep and bear arms is retained"? "Certainly not" to "enable each member of the community to protect and defend by individual force his private rights against every illegal invasion." The reason: The point of organizing governments was to displace private remedies for private violence with public ones. What did the Second Amendment and parallel state provisions do? They gave people a right to keep and bear arms for the purpose of participating in the armed militia, which could "resist, successfully, the effort of those who should conspire to overthrow the established institutions of the country, or subjugate their common liberties." As in *Aymette*, the court rejected a strong individual-rights view of the Second Amendment in favor of a militia-connected right. And, as in *Aymette*, the court did not distinguish between the state-organized select militia and the armed citizenry in general.

These developments reveal a change in the balance between the individual-rights and collective-rights views of Second Amendment. It's easy enough to read the cases, as the OLC memorandum does, to be consistent with the Standard Model. Gun-rights proponents could accurately describe these developments as dicta that implicitly recognize a citizen's right to keep and bear arms for purposes of resisting tyranny and for self-defense when governments fail to live up to their duty to provide protection. A full-fledged defense of the view that the Second Amendment merely protected state-organized militias against disarmament by the national government had not yet been articulated. Still, bits and pieces that eventually could be assembled into such a defense were accumulating during the nineteenth century. The collective-rights view was pretty clearly gaining purchase in the legal community.

The U.S. Supreme Court provided another piece for the collective-rights mosaic in 1886. Proponents of gun rights point to the role of black militias in resisting the Ku Klux Klan's depredations during Reconstruction to support their claim that the Fourteenth Amendment gave everyone a federal constitutional right, enforceable against state laws, to keep and bear arms. The Supreme Court rejected the argument that the Fourteenth Amendment incorporated the Bill of Rights, including the Second Amendment, in two steps. The Fourteenth Amendment says, "No state shall make or enforce any law which shall abridge the privileges or immunities of citizens of the United States." In the *Slaughterhouse Cases*, decided in 1873, the Court held that this clause did not make the Bill of Rights enforceable against state laws. The clause protected only rights that were somehow associated especially with citizenship of the United States, such as the right to travel to the nation's capital. One reason Justice Samuel Miller gave for this narrow holding was that a broad reading would transfer enormous power, previously held only by state legislatures, to Congress and to the federal courts. Justice Miller could not believe that the Fourteenth Amendment's adopters wanted to do so.

The *Slaughterhouse Cases* held out the possibility that *specific* rights listed in the Bill of Rights might be enforceable against the states if they could be described as rights associated with national citizenship. The Court addressed the question of whether the Second Amendment was such a right in the 1886 case of *Presser v. Illinois*. Germans who emigrated to the United States created a large number of civic associations, many of which re-created in the United States the kinds of physical and quasi-military training they were familiar with from Germany. Herman Presser helped run the "Lehr und Wehr Verein" in Illinois, an association devoted, its charter said, to "improving the mental and bodily condition of its members, so as to qualify them for the duties of a citizen of the republic." In 1879 Presser led a march of about 400 Verein members through Chicago's streets, riding horses and carrying rifles and swords.

This sounds like a group organizing itself as a citizen militia. But there's more to the story. "Lehr und Wehr Verein" translates as "Study and Self-Defense Association," and Presser's group was also an organization of German socialists, some of whom became active in Chicago's anarchist community. (Eventually some of the members were implicated in the Haymarket Massacre of 1886, facing perhaps trumped-up charges of murdering a policeman.) Illinois's legislature responded to these German-American associations—or militias, or gun clubs—by outlawing them. A statute adopted in 1879 made it illegal for a group "to associate themselves together as a military company or organization, or to drill or parade with arms" without a state-granted license—other than members of "the regular organized volunteer militia." Presser appealed his conviction for violating this statute to the Supreme Court.

Justice William Woods gave two reasons for rejecting Presser's argument that his conviction violated the Second Amendment. First, the Fourteenth Amendment did not incorporate the Second Amendment. The right "to associate with others as a military company" was not a privilege or immunity of United States citizens. Justice Woods observed that "all citizens capable of bearing arms constitute the reserve militia of the United States as well as of the States." This implied that the states could not "prohibit the people from keeping and bearing arms, so as to deprive the United States of their rightful resource for maintaining the public security, and disable the people from performing their duty to the general government."

Justice Woods's second reason was more straightforward. In a single sentence, he wrote that laws "which only forbid bodies of men to associate together as military organizations ... unless authorized by law, do not infringe the right of the people to keep and bear arms." What this says is that states can outlaw citizen militias without violating the Second Amendment—a position in some tension with Justice Woods's view that states can't regulate weapons possession in ways that interfere with the national government's interest in defending the nation. What Justice Woods wrote, though, simply *is* the states' rights position on the Second Amendment's meaning.

Justice Woods's statement was clearly dictum, and unsupported by any reasoning. It did not resolve the recurrent questions of the amendment's meaning, but it did contribute yet another piece in support of the states' rights interpretation. And importantly, treating the question of incorporation as easy and obvious flows quite naturally from the collective-rights interpretation of the Second Amendment: Incorporation would mean that the Second Amendment's prohibition, whatever it is, applies to state governments. But according to Justice Woods, state laws against private militias like Presser's didn't violate the right to keep and bear arms. That right—that is, the Second Amendment—could apply *only* to state-organized militias. And yet it makes no sense at all to say that states are barred from regulating the activities of militias that they themselves organize. Justice Woods's approach turns the Second Amendment's focus from the right to keep and bear arms to the state's power to regulate its own militia.

The only other Supreme Court decision discussing the Second Amendment in any detail is *United States v. Miller* (1939). Jack Miller was indicted for violating the National Firearms Act of

1934 by possessing a sawed-off shotgun. The trial judge dismissed the indictment, finding that the statute violated the Second Amendment. Miller's lawyers didn't even put in an appearance at the Supreme Court, which, in a short opinion issued six weeks after the case was argued, unanimously upheld the statute. Justice James McReynolds's opinion cited the Aymette decision in support of his central conclusion:

> In the absence of any evidence tending to show that possession or use of a [sawed-off shotgun] at this time has some reasonable relationship to the preservation or efficiency of a well regulated militia, we cannot say that the Second Amendment guarantees the right to keep and bear such an instrument. Certainly it is not within judicial notice that this weapon is any part of the ordinary military equipment or that its use could contribute to the common defense.

The test here is weapons-specific: Congress can outlaw the possession of weapons that are not reasonably understood to be part of the ordinary equipment of the regular military.

Justice McReynolds described the militia as "all males physically capable of acting in concert for the common defense." But in describing the Second Amendment in more detail, he seemingly qualified this citizen-oriented definition with one more focused on state-organized militias. The paragraph doing so began by citing the constitutional provision for placing militias under national control, with its reference to the role of the states in organizing such militias by appointing its officers and training its members. Justice McReynolds observed that the Second Amendment "must be interpreted and applied" with reference to its "obvious purpose," which was, he wrote, "to assure the continuation and render possible the effectiveness of *such forces*." I've added the italics to emphasize the intrusion here of a reference to the state-organized militias.

As of 2007, *Miller* was the Supreme Court's most recent decision dealing expressly with the Second Amendment's meaning. I was tempted to call it the Court's most recent extended discussion of the Second Amendment, but the opinion is so short that it really can't be called extended. As with essentially all the post-founding material, *Miller* has two strands. The dominant one gives a sense—no more than that, and certainly not a holding—that there's something mistaken about the Standard Model's interpretation of the Second Amendment, and that something like a states' rights interpretation better captures the amendment's meaning. The other strand continues to refer to the militia as the armed citizenry generally.

Gun-rights proponents take from *Miller* the proposition that the Second Amendment protects a gun-owner's right to own a weapon that *is* "part of the ordinary military equipment," but that's clearly an over-reading of the opinion. All the Supreme Court said was that a sawed-off shotgun was not "part of the ordinary military equipment," which implies only that it's an open question whether the Second Amendment gives the individual a right to own weapons that might be ordinary military equipment. And even if the Supreme Court eventually adopts the gun-rights reading of *Miller*, it would still have to decide what weapons fell within the protected category: Small concealable handguns ("Saturday night specials")? Machine guns? What else?

If you paid close attention, you could have caught a quick glimpse of *Miller* during the confirmation hearings for Supreme Court justice Samuel Alito. Opponents of his nomination tried to get some mileage out of the fact that as a circuit court judge he had dissented from a decision upholding a conviction of a firearms dealer for possessing machine guns. Then-Judge Alito relied on a recent Supreme Court decision holding that Congress couldn't use its power to regulate commerce among the several states to prohibit the possession of guns near schools; Judge Alito argued that the logic of that decision extended to laws banning possession of machine guns. His colleagues on the bench disagreed with him, and so had to take up the defendant's argument that the statute violated the Second Amendment. It didn't, they said, because, like the sawed-off shotgun in *Miller*, machine guns don't have a reasonable relationship to "the preservation or efficiency of a well regulated militia."

By the middle of the twentieth century, the clear tendency in the law was against the Standard Model and in favor of some collective-rights interpretation. Since *Miller* the Supreme Court has assiduously avoided taking up Second Amendment cases.

In 1981 the village of Morton Grove, a suburb of Chicago, adopted a complete ban on handgun possession within the town limits. Town council members said they were concerned about recent assassination attempts on President Ronald Reagan and Pope John Paul II, and were provoked into action when some of their constituents complained about a businessman's plan to open a gun shop in the town, which already had a store selling rifles and shotguns. One council member voted against the possession ban because he thought it violated the right to bear arms, and another because she didn't want to spend money defending the ordinance against the inevitable legal challenge. Victor Quilici, who participated in pistol-shooting competitions, filed the lawsuit on the same day the ordinance was adopted.

The trial judge rejected Quilici's claims, and he appealed. A lawyer, Quilici represented himself, with the assistance of Don Kates, a prominent gun-rights advocate. Morton Grove's ordinance was the first complete ban on gun possession ever enacted in the United States, and Quilici's lawsuit attracted the attention of gun-rights and gun-control proponents alike. Handgun Control—later renamed the Brady Campaign to Prevent Gun Violence—filed a brief supporting the town, the Illinois State Rifle Association opposed it, and a coalition of eleven states tried to get the case dismissed without a ruling on the merits. The court of appeals had little difficulty upholding the ordinance.

Most of the court's opinion dealt with Illinois state law. Judge William Bauer did offer two responses to Quilici's Second Amendment arguments. He adopted the states' rights interpretation: "the right to bear arms is inextricably connected to the preservation of a militia." He cited *Miller* for the proposition that the right "extends only to those arms which are necessary to maintain a well regulated militia," and, in a footnote, said that "we do not consider individually owned handguns to be military weapons." It's fair to describe this analysis as cursory.

But the Supreme Court's decision in *Presser* that the Second Amendment didn't limit state or local power was an insurmountable hurdle. Quilici argued that by the 1970s the Court had repudiated the holding of the *Slaughterhouse Cases* that the Fourteenth Amendment didn't incorporate the Bill of Rights, through selective incorporation. One after another, the Court had held, particular provisions of the Bill of Rights—free speech, the privilege against self-incrimination, the ban on excessive bail, and more—had been applied to the states. The time had come, Quilici argued, to do the same for the Second Amendment. Judge Bauer responded that the Supreme Court continued to cite *Presser* approvingly, including one case that selectively incorporated *another* Bill of Rights protection in the Fourteenth Amendment. And in any event, overturning *Presser* was for the Supreme Court, not a lower court.

So Quilici tried to get the Supreme Court to reverse the court of appeals, again with significant support from gun-rights groups. Without comment, the Supreme Court refused to hear the case.

Along with statutes that deny access to weapons to some people but not others, which I discuss below, laws completely banning gun possession are probably the most constitutionally vulnerable ones imaginable. If the courts uphold such a law, they ought to uphold *any* gun-control law. Yet, the decision upholding the Morton Grove ordinance didn't open the floodgates. The District of Columbia *has* adopted a complete ban on handgun possession, which is under a constitutional cloud as I write, but no other major cities or states have. One reason for legislative inaction, of course, is the political clout of gun-rights proponents, including the National Rifle Association. Another, though, is that localized gun-control policies might not make a lot of sense. As the mayor of one town that banned gun sales observed, "Residents could go to the next village and buy a gun and we would have no qualms about it." This leakage means that only reasonably comprehensive gun-control proposals hold out the prospect of having some real effect on reducing gun violence, and such proposals attract the greatest political opposition precisely because of their scope. (We'll examine whether even such proposals do much good or bad in Chapter 4.)

Banning possession of rifles is politically infeasible, and banning possession of handguns has proven to be so as well. Gun-control proponents have found another target—"assault weapons." Many cities have banned possession of those weapons, though coming up with a legally workable definition of "assault weapons" is trickier than you might think. On January 17, 1989, in Stockton, California, Patrick Purdy killed five elementary schoolchildren and wounded twenty-nine others when he fired an AK-47 semi-automatic weapon on them during their morning recess. Meeting in a special session, the California legislature responded with the Roberti-Roos Assault Weapons Control Act. The act banned the possession of assault weapons. How did it identify what an assault weapon was? By naming more than seventy-five specific types of weapons, by manufacturer's name and model number. The possibilities for evading that ban are obvious (reincorporate yourself under another name and make a new model of assault weapon), and manufacturers seized them. So a decade later the act was amended to identify some general characteristics of assault weapons. *That* list has eight sections, some with four, five, and six subsections. An example: "(4) A semiautomatic pistol that has the capacity to accept a detachable magazine and . . . [a] shroud that is attached to, or partially or completely encircles, the barrel that allows the bearer to fire the weapon without burning his or her hand, except a slide that encloses the barrel." Here too the opportunities for redesign seem substantial. Seeking to ban "assault weapons" may give some politicians valuable benefits, but it is not a promising legislative strategy.

In February 2000, a group of California residents who owned or wanted to buy weapons classified as assault weapons by the act filed a federal lawsuit, claiming that the act violated the Second Amendment. Federal courts are divided into geographical "circuits," and California is in the Ninth Circuit, at the time probably the nation's most liberal federal appeals court. The case was heard by three judges: Frank Magill, a judge appointed by Ronald Reagan who usually sat in North Dakota but had a temporary assignment to the Ninth Circuit; Raymond Fisher, who served in the Clinton administration before his appointment; and Stephen Reinhardt, perhaps the most liberal federal appeals court judge in the country.

Judge Reinhardt took the opportunity provided by the challenge to the Roberti-Roos Act to participate in what he called "a robust constitutional debate" over the Second Amendment's meaning. He found that the "collective rights model," which "guarantees the right of the people to maintain effective state militias," offered "the best interpretation of the Second Amendment." His opinion rehearsed the arguments we've already laid out, and found the Roberti-Roos Act entirely constitutional. The statute's challengers asked the entire court of appeals to consider the case, but they fell short. Judges Alex Kozinski and Andrew Kleinfeld, both noted conservative judges appointed to the bench by President Reagan, wrote dissents criticizing Judge Reinhardt's position and laying out the Standard Model. Yet, indicating that the arguments are not entirely congruent with ordinary political labels, they were joined in their support for the Standard Model by judges appointed by Presidents Jimmy Carter and Bill Clinton. Despite the case's prominence, the Supreme Court declined to review Judge Reinhardt's decision.

Look at the pattern revealed by statutes and cases since the 1850s: A substantial body of laws regulating weapons possession and a small number of opinions addressing Second Amendment objections to such laws, with no opinions from appellate courts invalidating any modern regulations, and an apparent lack of interest by the Supreme Court in taking fundamental Second Amendment questions. The pattern suggests that we have a tradition in which the Second Amendment imposes at most extremely weak, perhaps indiscernible, limitations on the government's power to regulate the use and possession of weapons of any sort.

Why should these developments matter? Gun-rights proponents point out, accurately, that the collective-rights view is a latecomer to constitutional interpretation. When the Second Amendment was adopted, the collective-rights view, to the extent that anyone held it, was a minor theme in contrast to the stronger citizen-rights one. So, gun-rights proponents argue, the later interpretation should be rejected in favor of the one more faithful to the original understanding. For someone like me, who comes to the Second Amendment from a more general interest in the Constitution as a whole, what is most striking about discussions of the amendment is that most of them stop with textual and originalist inquiries. The nineteenth- and twentieth-century developments we've seen in this chapter mean that gun-rights proponents can prevail only by fighting the interpretive battle solely on textual and originalist grounds. A minor puzzle is why gun-control proponents think they should fight on those same grounds. They *do* have some evidence they can use from originalist materials, but the later developments give them much more ammunition.

The relation between originalist interpretation and the use of other legal arguments raises deep and complicated issues of constitutional theory, and I can only sketch the outlines of the arguments here. Turn aside from the Second Amendment, and examine how constitutional law treats other constitutional provisions. The First Amendment provides a dramatic and useful example. There is no doubt about what people understood in 1791 as the meaning of the First Amendment's prohibition of laws "abridging the freedom of speech." It meant that Congress could not enact laws imposing "prior restraints" on speech or publication through a licensing or similar system, but it did *not* prohibit Congress from enacting laws that would punish speech after it occurred. And Congress happily did so, enacting the Sedition Act of 1798, which made it a crime to publish "false, scandalous and malicious" statements about the national government or the president. As with the Second Amendment, so too with the First: The experience of the 1790s led to a new understanding of the First Amendment's point in the new republic. The Sedition Act was aimed at supporters of Vice President Thomas Jefferson (notably, the act didn't make it a crime to publish malicious statements about *him*), and Jeffersonians endorsed a more libertarian theory that had been gaining adherents in the 1790s. Constitutional practice took a while to catch up with theory, and governments regulated speech in ways quite inconsistent with modern understandings of the free speech principle through the early or middle of the twentieth century. Today, though, we have strong protections for speech—far stronger than the generation that adopted the First Amendment thought that amendment required.

Other than academics obsessed with "theory" and op-ed writers trying to push an agenda, almost no one today argues for a return to the original understanding of the First Amendment. Conservatives, for example, advocate giving commercial advertising protection almost as strong as that given political speech, even though no one seriously contends that in 1791 *anyone* thought that the First Amendment protected commercial advertising at all. The reason is that original understandings matter for constitutional interpretation, but so do tradition and precedent. As Justice Antonin Scalia has put it, he and most proponents of a jurisprudence of original understanding are "faint-hearted." Their originalism yields when tradition and precedent weigh heavily against what inquiries into original understandings reveal.

Justice Stephen Breyer's description of how most lawyers and judges actually *do* constitutional law also describes how gun-control proponents approach constitutional interpretation:

> They read the text's language along with related language in other parts of the document. They take account of its history, including history that shows what the language likely meant to those who wrote it. They look to tradition indicating how the relevant language was, and is, used in the law. They examine

precedents interpreting the phrase, holding or suggesting what the phrase means and how it has been applied. They try to understand the phrase's purposes or ... the values it embodies, and they consider the likely consequences of the interpretive alternatives, valued in terms of the phrase's purposes.

Gun-control proponents rely on an approach to constitutional interpretation that gives original understanding some weight, but gives even more to tradition and precedent. That approach is well-grounded in constitutional theory—indeed, probably better grounded than originalism itself. One study published in 1991, for example, compared the references to original understandings and to precedents in constitutional opinions by Chief Justice Rehnquist and Justice William Brennan, one usually described as sympathetic to originalism, the other not. Rehnquist referred to originalist materials in about 10 percent of his argument, Brennan in about 6 percent. These references were massively outweighed by the references to precedent—at 80 percent for both of them. Even if we double or triple the percentage of originalist arguments, we're still left with a heavy preponderance of *other* interpretive methods. And, if you adopt an approach that brings in more than originalism—as the Supreme Court plainly does—the collective-rights view is at least as plausible an interpretation as the citizen-rights view.

How does the proposal that gun owners have to pass a licensing test fare under the collective-rights view? The answer is obvious: A licensing test—and, indeed, many more and more extensive regulations—is just fine, because, under the collective-rights view, people do not have a constitutional right to own guns independent of their participation in the organized militia. From the collective-rights point of view, the right to own a gun is just like the right to drive a car—something the government can regulate pretty much however it wants. The collective-rights view places a great deal of weight on the history of firearms regulation and on the policy justifications for regulating gun ownership. That history and—perhaps—policy considerations support the argument that the licensing-test proposal is constitutional under the collective-rights view.

In this chapter and the ones before, I've tried to present the best cases for the gun-rights and gun-control positions on the Second Amendment's meaning. I've also tried to indicate where each side's case is weak and how advocates attempt to deal with weaknesses, because dealing with weaknesses is an important part of advocacy too. What's the bottom line? On balance, originalism supports some version of an individual-rights interpretation, although the case for such an interpretation is closer than proponents of the gun-rights position acknowledge, and the states' rights interpretation preferred by gun-control advocates isn't entirely ruled out by originalist interpretation. Approaching the question of interpreting the Second Amendment as judges do—that is, by treating original meaning as important but taking other matters, such as precedent, into account—changes the bottom line. Gun-control proponents have a significantly stronger case than their adversaries if we treat the question of interpreting the Second Amendment as an ordinary constitutional question and use all the interpretive tools judges ordinarily use.

Of course when we think about gun rights and gun control outside the context of constitutional interpretation, we care about whether one or the other position will make our lives safer or more dangerous. Whether gun rights or gun control is good public policy is therefore part of any sensible analysis of the Second

Amendment's meaning. As it turns out, though, any gun-related policy that is likely to get through our political processes is unlikely to have much effect on public safety one way or the other. That conclusion, I argue in the next chapter, helps us understand the cultural clash that really underlies the heated controversy over the Second Amendment's meaning. To see why, though, we need to examine some prominent policy proposals.

CHAPTER FOUR

Gun Control and Public Policy

GUN-CONTROL AND gun-rights advocates circulate dueling anecdotes to bolster their positions. Here are some, gathered from
the websites of the National Rifle Association and the Brady
Campaign to Prevent Gun Violence.

- Khalid Ali's family moved from Najaf, Iraq, to get away
from that nation's violence. They relocated to Buffalo, New York,
where Khalid made new friends. One, Norma Geil's fifteen-year-
old daughter (whose name was unpublished because she was a
juvenile), invited the eighteen-year-old Khalid and about thirty
other friends to a raucous birthday party on Saturday, February 11,
2006. There was a lot of drinking and marijuana smoking; four
kids were asked to leave the party, and as they did six others
followed them outside and robbed them. The party continued
into Sunday afternoon. The few still there got hold of several
weapons. Geil's daughter was waving around a rifle that she
thought was unloaded, when it went off. The shot hit Khalid in

his head, killing him. Norma Geil was charged with child en-
dangerment (she had been at the party, and police said that she
had required the party's guests to supply money, alcohol, or drugs
to get in). Her daughter was charged with juvenile delinquency.

- On Thursday morning, February 24, 2005, Thomas Sampson showed up late for work on repairing a bridge in Los Angeles.
Rene Flores, his boss, chewed him out over the telephone. Sampson spent the day getting angrier and angrier. Late in the afternoon he abandoned his city-owned truck on a freeway, took a
bus and got his car, and drove home. He changed from his work
clothes into a suit—and picked up an AK-47 assault rifle. He drove
to Flores's office and shot him. Ricardo Garris, Flores's assistant,
happened to be in the office, and he too was killed. Sampson then
drove to a police station and turned himself in.

- Barron Whiteman walked into the "Off the Wagon" bar in
Philadelphia at about 1:30 in the morning, just before closing time.
After about a half hour, Whiteman shouted that everyone—the
four customers and the staff—should "hit the floor," and started
firing. One of his bullets hit bartender Natalie Biggs in the hip.
Whiteman's gun jammed, which gave Biggs a chance to pull out a
.38 revolver, a gun that's sometimes described as a classic "ladies'
gun." She shot Whiteman, who stumbled out of the bar. Shortly
afterward, the police found Whiteman slumped behind the wheel
of his car, a few blocks from the bar. They took him to a nearby
hospital, where he was pronounced dead.

I have no doubt that these accounts are accurate; indeed, I've
filled in some details by tracking down the original news reports
on which the advocacy groups relied. The real question, though,
is what these anecdotes tell us about good gun policy.

To the Brady Campaign, Khalid Ali's death shows the need for
"safe storage" laws, which require adults to store loaded guns in a

place that is reasonably inaccessible to children, or use a device to lock the gun. To the NRA, safe storage laws slow down the access to guns whose display or use might scare off a rapist or burglar. To gun-control proponents, workplace shootings with AK-47 rifles show the need for bans on private ownership of such deadly weapons. To the NRA, weapon-specific bans are pointless because they sweep in weapons that responsible gun hobbyists can use for entirely lawful purposes and because they can be evaded without much difficulty. As we saw in Chapter 2, California had already made it illegal to own AK-47 rifles, but Sampson had one anyway.

Anecdotes can motivate members of interest groups to pressure their legislators. Good policy, though, requires some understanding of the overall effects of different rules. But, as we'll see, controversy over what the evidence shows about such effects is as deep as controversy over the Second Amendment's meaning. The reason is that differences over gun policy result from differences over our understanding of who we are as Americans. They reflect *cultural* differences more than merely policy disagreement or disagreements between "red state" Republicans and "blue state" Democrats. And the same is true about disagreements about the Second Amendment's meaning. I concluded Chapter 1 by describing Natty Bumppo in the *Leatherstocking Tales*. There he served as a symbol of armed resistance to an oppressive government. But he is also a cultural icon, someone who figures in the way some Americans think about what "America" is. The Second Amendment has become one of the focal points of the culture war over defining America.

We're about to examine three policies prominent in contemporary discussions of gun policy: "must issue" laws requiring that local law enforcement officials issue licenses to carry concealed weapons, "safe storage" laws requiring that guns be kept locked up at home, and enhanced enforcement of existing gun-control laws. Before that, though, there's a preliminary question. Even if these policies worked to reduce crime in general or gun violence, how *much* would they do? Frank Zimring, who has studied crime and violence in the United States and elsewhere for more than thirty years, describes what he calls the "free-lunch syndrome," a "tendency to couple small operational changes with the full weight of firearms control symbolism." Those who support what to an outsider seems like small policy changes "suggest[] that their passage will have a substantial impact on rates of lethal violence."

Consider here two policies we looked at in Chapter 3: local bans on gun sales or possession, and bans on particularly disfavored weapons. Supporters and opponents invest enormous energy in fighting over such proposals, and yet there are obvious reasons to question whether anything much would change were such policies to be adopted. The problem, as we saw, is leakage: You can't buy a gun in one suburb? Drive fifteen miles and find a gun dealer there. Define the disfavored weapon however you want, and gun-makers will be able to design around the definition, achieving the same level of lethality (or more) with a weapon that costs no more than the banned one and that doesn't fit the statutory definition.

Even so, large-scale legislative and litigation campaigns focus on adopting local bans and prohibiting disfavored weapons. Perhaps we ought to look at these campaigns not in terms of public policy directly, but in terms what the interest groups who take part in them get out of them: Whatever the policy value of the proposals, they certainly are good fund-raising devices: They help one side raise money nominally to get the policy adopted, and help the other side raise money nominally to block the policy's adoption—but mostly, I suspect, to pay the salaries of the interest groups' staffs.

The 2006 NRA policy du jour, for example, was advocacy of statutes described by supporters as "stand your ground" laws and by opponents as "shoot first" laws. These statutes deal with the rules for criminal cases in which a home owner is charged with using deadly force against an intruder who threatened his property but not his life. The traditional rule expresses a preference for life over property: The home owner can't use deadly force until his life is threatened. "Stand your ground" laws change that rule to let the home owner draw a gun and shoot an intruder who isn't yet posing any threat to his life. Whatever you think of these statutes, you have to realize that they deal with an incredibly small part of the universe of crime. That they've become the focus of legislative campaigns indicates to me that interest groups care about keeping the waters roiling so they can raise money at least as much as they care about making good public policy. Still, people do give them money for these campaigns, which indicates that something else—I'll argue, a cultural struggle over national self-definition—is at stake.

One gun policy *might* have a big impact on gun-related violence, at least eventually: a nationwide ban on the private ownership of guns, coupled with a policy of confiscating all guns already in private possession. Even that policy wouldn't have an immediate effect, given how many guns there are in the United States, and the likely low level of effectiveness of the confiscation policy. But more important, as a political matter there is no chance whatever that such a ban will be enacted. With that policy off the table, we are left with smaller interventions as realistic policy options.

In thinking about gun policy, how can we know whether any policy "works"?

Usually, we begin with some sort of intuitive theory about why it *might* work. For "safe storage" laws, for example, the theory is that when kids can't easily get at guns in their houses, they won't shoot the guns accidentally or commit suicide with them; for "must issue" laws, the theory is that a person thinking about robbing someone will think twice if he has to worry that his intended victim might be carrying a concealed weapon. Then we compare how much gun violence there was before we started to use the policy to the amount of gun violence afterward. We'll conclude that the policy worked if the level goes down in a way that makes sense in light of our intuitive theory about why it might work. This process is open to criticism at three points: the theory, the test for importance, and the facts. It turns out that, at least where gun policy is involved, people who don't like the conclusions they're reading have been able to develop serious criticisms at each point.

Begin with the theory. We "explain" the drop in gun violence by our intuitive theory, but we really don't know what kids actually did at home or what potential criminals actually thought. All we have are the statistics about violence—the product of decisions made by huge numbers of people in all sorts of situations, Social scientists deal with this problem by creating "models" of human behavior. They say, in words I've invented,

Suppose you knew how many men and women, older people and young people, and so on, were in their homes, on the streets, driving their cars, and so on, and each one faced some risk of meeting up with a potential criminal, some men, some women, some old, some young, and each potential criminal could guess the chance that the intended victim was carrying a concealed weapon. Given these assumptions, how much gun violence would you end up seeing? And then, keeping everything else the same, we put a "must issue" law in place. That would increase the chances that the potential

[78]

victims were carrying concealed weapons. Given our assumptions, how much would that change decrease the amount
of gun violence? And, finally, how well does our prediction
about the change match up with what we've actually seen?

This modeling and matching is done by social scientists who
travel as "econometricians."

All this is sensible enough in the classroom, but it's incredibly
difficult to pull off in practice. Offering a skeptical comment
about efforts by econometricians to use their skills in debates
about public policy, George Stigler, a winner of the Nobel Me-
morial Prize for Economic Science, published a satirical paper,
"The Conference Handbook," giving economists a checklist of
criticisms they could offer whenever *anyone* delivered a paper.
One concludes, "The specification of the model is incorrect." The
point here is that you can always criticize the assumptions that are
built into the model someone else uses to explain the effects of
the policy change you're both interested in.

To take an example that's going to come up in my discussion
of policy choices: Many of the policies of interest today were put
into place in the early to mid-1990s, and soon afterward the ju-
risdictions that adopted them did indeed experience sharp drops
in crime. Did the policies "work" to reduce crime and violence?
Maybe not. Because, just at the time the policies were adopted,
the crack epidemic, which was itself strongly associated with violent crime, hit its peak. The drop-off in crime and violence in the
late 1990s might have occurred if no policies changed at all.

This is an incredibly simple example, and it's easy enough to
deal with—at least in theory. In connection with "must issue"
laws, for example, researcher John Lott said in effect, "Well, let's
assume that crack-related violence was associated with urban areas, and let's try to find two urban areas next to each other, but

separated by a state border. With any luck, one state will have adopted a 'must issue' law while the other didn't. If so, let's see if we can find out whether the level of crime and violence dropped more where the state had a 'must issue' law even as crime and violence were dropping everywhere because crack-related violence was receding." And, he said, when you did that test, you actually saw crime dropping in the "must issue" city and rising in the other. One challenge addressed—but there are always more, as Stigler knew.

Econometricians use a number of statistical techniques to test what they call the "robustness" of their results to small changes in the model specification. And, unfortunately, sometimes one "robustness" test makes the model look pretty good, while another makes it look pretty bad. Again, in the "must issue" policy debate, one prominent criticism of Lott's study is that the results favorable to "must issue" disappear if you take Florida out of the database. The authors who made that argument point out as well that looking at results for different states yields odd results: "Murders decline in Florida but increase in West Virginia. Assaults fall in Maine but increase in Pennsylvania." Gently commenting on the intuitive theory that underlies the "must issue" argument, they observe, "We doubt that any model of criminal behavior could account for the variation we observe." And using Stigler's phrase, they conclude, "Widely varying estimates such as these are classic evidence that...the model is misspecified."

Another Nobel Prize winner, Milton Friedman, provides a second skeptical view of econometric studies. Remember, at the end of all the model specification and data crunching, we want to know how introducing the new policy affected crime and violence. Social scientists ask, "Now that we've seen a difference in outcomes in the 'must issue' states and the others, how likely is it that, given all the elements of our model, the difference in outcomes resulted from the difference in policy?" They say that a difference in outcomes is *statistically significant* if the odds are pretty small that the difference was just a random event, when you take everything into account. Friedman, though, is skeptical about resting too much on findings of statistical significance: "I have long had relatively little faith in judging statistical results by formal tests of statistical significance. I believe that it is much more important to base conclusions on a wide range of evidence coming from different sources over a long period of time." There's a technical and a practical reason for Friedman's skepticism. Technically, if your study is big enough—if, as social scientists put it, you get a large enough number of observations—you can generate results that satisfy the formal requirements of statistical significance almost at will. And practically, there's no necessary connection between statistical significance, a purely mathematical concept, and social importance, even though it's easy for ordinary citizens to confuse the two. As one online source puts it, "[S]uppose we give 1,000 people an IQ test, and we ask if there is a significant difference between male and female scores. The mean score for males is 98 and the mean score for females is 100." It turns out that using a standard technique, that difference is statistically significant. "The big question is, 'So what?' The difference between 98 and 100 on an IQ test is . . . so small . . . that it[']s not even important."

And finally, there are the facts. Everyone in the field knows that there's a lot we don't know: Statistics on homicides are pretty good, because bodies turn up (most of the time). Statistics on other crimes are not nearly as accurate. Social scientists rarely use numbers based on crimes reported to the police because they are pretty confident that lots of people don't report crimes like assaults or even low-value robberies. The alternative is to use numbers based on surveys that ask people whether they were the victims of specific crimes, within some recent period. Social scientists think that these numbers are more accurate, but you wouldn't want to bet large amounts of money on the proposition that the survey results describe the "real" levels of crime and violence. Often enough, though, we're interested in trends— whether the teen suicide rate went up or stayed the same after a "safe storage" law was adopted—and, assuming that the inaccuracies in our factual inquiries haven't changed in the same period, we might be able to make some headway in policy analysis. But not if what we're looking for happen to be relatively rare events. Then, even if we ask a reasonably large number of people, we're going to come up with pretty large variations from one survey to the next.

Finding out even roughly what the relevant facts are is tricky. It would be nice to know, for example, how often people use their guns *safely*—not for hunting, but for defending themselves. If such uses are common and work to prevent crime, limiting gun ownership might be a bad idea; if they are rare or end up with lots of accidental or mistaken shootings, stronger gun controls might be justified. So how many defensive gun uses are there each year?

The figure most prominently quoted is that Americans use guns defensively 2.5 million times a year. That number comes from a survey aimed at finding out specifically about defensive gun uses that asked about 5,000 people, "Within the past five years, have you yourself or another member of your household used a gun, even if it was not fired, for self-protection or for the protection of property at home, work, or elsewhere?" Two hundred and thirteen people said, "Yes." After some reasonable numerical manipulations—multiplying the survey responses by appropriate population figures, dividing to get an annual figure— the authors came up with 2.5 million.

A study published three years later, based on surveys of crime victims generally, came up with a dramatically different number: 116,000 defensive gun uses a year. How can two surveys come up with such different results? The second survey asked a different question of a different group of people: People who first said that they had been the victims of various crimes or attempted crimes during the prior six months were then asked, "Was there anything you did or tried to do about the incident while it was going on? Did you do anything (else) with the idea of protecting yourself or your property while the incident was going on?" Notice the difference in the questions: The first survey asked about events over the past five years, long enough for memories about details to have faded, the second about the past six months; the first asked specifically about gun use—which might have induced the victim to provide a positive answer, or reminded the victim of the gun use—while the second was more open-ended.

Another clue to the difference in results comes from yet a third survey. This one found defensive uses in 322,000 rapes—which seems roughly consistent with a high number of uses for all crimes—but with "a 95 percent confidence interval of [12,000 to 632,000]." The "confidence interval" is a statistical measure that indicates what answers you're likely to get if you repeat the survey selecting the same number of people to ask from the same larger group. So, for this survey, if you repeated it again and again, nearly all of the time you'd get an answer between 12,000 and 632,000 annual defensive gun uses in rapes. As two statisticians put it, "A very wide interval may indicate that more data should be collected before anything very definite can be said about the parameter"—here, the actual number of defensive gun uses. It's not at all clear that we know much more after the survey than we did before.

Critics of the high estimate of defensive gun uses suggest that people respond to survey questions by saying that they used a gun even if they didn't. Being a crime victim (and getting included in a random survey sample) is rare for most of us, and, according to one critic, "[s]elf-report surveys...can wildly overestimate rare events which have some social desirability." Think about someone who was in a bar fight four years before the survey, and remembers—accurately or not—brandishing a handgun. He may have actually started the fight, but the odds are quite high, I suspect, that he'll say that he was the victim of an attempted assault, which he deterred by using his gun. "Whether one is a defender...or a perpetrator...may depend on perspective." In one telephone survey, thirteen people said that they had brandished a gun defensively, and thirty-eight said that someone else had "displayed" a gun against them "in a hostile manner." The authors wonder how many of the thirty-eight brandishers—who of course weren't in the survey—would have said that they used the gun defensively.

Another indication of some problems with the high-end estimates is the 322,000 uses in rapes and attempted rapes. The authors of *that* survey, who stand behind their statistical techniques, observe that that figure "is more than the total number of rapes and attempted rapes estimated from the best available source," crime victimization surveys. Of course, the latter surveys might be wrong too, but the errors would have to be really large for the 322,000 figure to correspond to reality. Similarly, their survey suggested that about "132,000 perpetrators were either wounded or killed at the hands of armed civilians in 1994." But, they noted, that's "just about the same as the total of all people who were shot and killed or received treatment for nonfatal gunshot wounds in an emergency room that year—yet we know that almost all of those are there" because they were victims of crime, accidents, or suicide attempts. Again, maybe the wounded criminals weren't hurt that badly or found treatment elsewhere than emergency rooms. But again, the chances are that the discrepancy arises because the estimate of defensive gun uses is wrong.

The National Academy of Sciences, through its research council, set up a committee "to improve research information and data on firearms." The committee's report stated, mildly, that the differences in estimates of defensive gun uses were "potentially troubling." Others were more skeptical, calling the 2.5 million figure "the gun debate's new mythical number." The real answer is that we have no idea how often guns are brandished in self-defense.

What was the National Academy of Sciences committee's overall conclusion? "[A]nswers to some of the most pressing questions cannot be addressed with existing data and research methods, however well designed....[T]he data available on [many] questions are too weak to support unambiguous conclusions or strong policy statements." That doesn't mean that people won't continue to rely on "facts" to justify their preferred policy proposals. It does mean that there won't be any real-world connection between the facts and the proposals. People will choose which facts they find persuasive on some basis other than "reality." The basis will be their understanding of who they are or want to be.

Let's examine three gun policies with that caution in mind: the "must issue" policy, "safe storage" laws, and law enforcement strategies that focus police effort on punishing criminals who use guns while committing their crimes. How can we know whether any of these policies "work"?

I'm going to spend a fair amount of space on the "more guns, less crime" theory because it's been the most important policy proposal offered by gun-rights advocates over the past decade, and because the empirical studies of the theory expose the general problems associated with assessing gun policy proposals. The theory is straightforward. John Lott, the theory's main proponent, was an economist working at the American Enterprise Institute, a conservative-leaning think tank, when he developed it. He adopted the standard economist's assumption that criminals are just like the rest of us. They think about what they might do over the next days or weeks, figure out what the costs and benefits of various choices would be, and choose the one that gives them the best prospect of the largest gain (taking costs and risks into account). So, if we increase the cost of engaging in crime, some potential criminals will decide that on balance they are better off abiding by the law. The benefits are what they will get away with if they succeed. The costs include the chance that they won't succeed. This includes the odds of being arrested and the chance that they will be thwarted in the middle of the "job." Criminals can be stopped when their intended victims resist, which they can do by pulling out a gun, threatening to shoot ("brandishing"), or actually shooting. The more potential victims who have guns, the greater the chance that someone chosen at random will have a gun, the more likely it is that a criminal will get hurt if he assaults someone, and so the less likely it is that a criminal will go after potential victims. So: "More Guns, Less Crime."

There are a couple of important tweaks to the theory. First, suppose not everyone has a gun, but everyone who does displays it openly. That improves the criminals' odds considerably. They can target victims who aren't displaying a gun. So, the theory continues, what matters is how many people are carrying *concealed* weapons. Uncertainty about whether a potential victim has a gun will factor into the criminal's calculation. If you're a potential criminal looking around for a target, the fact that there are more guns out there won't deter you if you know who has the guns; you'll just shift your target from someone who has a gun to someone who doesn't. This is the difference between using the Club in your car and the Lo-Jack system, where you're not allowed to say that your car has Lo-Jack installed. A thief who sees the Club in one car simply moves on to the next one. Thieves in cities with Lo-Jack don't know whether the car they've targeted has Lo-Jack, and so they'll steal fewer cars. Lott therefore examined what happened when people were allowed to carry *concealed* weapons.

Second, almost every state has laws authorizing police officials to issue permits to carry concealed weapons. Some state laws are discretionary, saying that police chiefs *can* issue permits to people who explain why they need to have a concealed weapon. Many police chiefs are quite skeptical about the explanations applicants offer, and in "may issue" states permits are rarely granted. In contrast, there are the "must issue" states. There police chiefs *must* give concealed-weapons permits to anyone who satisfies some fairly standard requirements (particularly, not having a criminal record).

The "more guns, less crime" argument is that "must issue" statutes are a really good idea because, unlike "may issue" statutes as they are actually administered, "must issue" statutes lead to an increase in the number of concealed weapons carried by law-abiding citizens and thereby really affect criminals' calculations about committing a crime. Or, more precisely, about committing a crime in which there's a chance that they'll run up against someone carrying a concealed weapon. So, the theory goes, in a "must issue" state, you should find crimes involving one-on-one confrontations—murders, rapes, assaults, robberies—decreasing.

"Must issue" rules might actually lead to increases in other crimes when criminals who otherwise would commit one-on-one crimes turn to "safer" crimes that involve much smaller risks of one-on-one confrontations: They will "case" a house to make sure that no one's home before they break in, or they'll steal a car from a garage rather than car-jacking it. Or they might lead to no effects on those other crimes, or decreases, as potential criminals do the calculations and decide that, all things considered, they can do better by being law abiding.

That's the theory, and it has a certain intuitive appeal. What Lott did—or, according to his critics, tried to do—was to show that the facts about criminal activity fit the theory. Relying on various statistics and mathematical calculations, he concluded that cities and states that *required* sheriffs to issue permits to carry concealed weapons unless they had a good reason to deny the permit had less crime than cities and states where sheriffs had discretion to issue such permits. Lott's strongest evidence came in a complicated analysis of crime statistics. He compiled numbers on crime rates in U.S. counties from 1977 to 1992 (later expanded through 1997). Then he looked at crime rates in each state with a "must issue" law, before and after the law went into effect. Of course, lots of things affect crime rates—how many young men there are in a state, how well the economy is doing, and more. So Lott "controlled" for those other things, using statistical techniques that are designed to single out the effects of the one thing you're interested in. All this goes into a mathematical "model"—the specification of which Stigler worried about.

Lott fed the crime rate data into the model he specified and came up with striking results: Adopting a "must issue" law had dramatically large effects in reducing violent crime, pretty much across the board. One of Lott's models had murder going down by about 8 percent, rape by about 5 percent, assaults by about 7 percent—and, consistent with one view of the underlying theory, property crimes and car thefts going up. Another model showed reductions in murder of about 4 percent and in rape of about 1.5 percent, with essentially no effects on other crimes. According to these numbers, if every state had a "must issue" law in 1992, there would have been 1,414 fewer homicides, 4,177 fewer rapes, and over 60,000 fewer assaults. As Lott put it, "Our evidence implies that concealed handguns are the most cost-effective method of reducing crime thus far analyzed by economists, providing a higher return than increased law enforcement or incarceration, other private security devices, or social programs like early educational intervention."

Sounds ideal—a low-cost, incredibly effective crime-prevention technique. Lott's initial article on "more guns, less crime" ran to sixty-eight pages, with eighteen tables and lots of discussion of possible problems with the statistics. What could be wrong with it? His critics said, Quite a bit.

Some of the criticisms are fairly technical, though their basics are easily understood. Using county-level information generates more data, which in itself increases the chance that the analysis will produce statistically significant results—without necessarily increasing the chance that it will produce practically significant ones. Lott's data had some "coding errors"—that is, he used inconsistent definitions of some terms (such as the dates when a "must issue" law went into effect) and entered the wrong information in some of his boxes. His response was reasonable: Even a few hundred small errors in a database with thousands of items isn't likely to affect the general picture he drew—although someone who acknowledged that kind of error shouldn't produce falsely precise numbers like "4,177 fewer rapes." And, it turns out, statisticians can show that the overall results *can* differ dramatically if a small number of mistakes are made in the right places in a large database.

According to critics, Lott's results were not robust. If you make reasonable changes in the underlying data—mostly dropping some states or changing the time period over which the effects are measured—you end up finding that adopting a "must issue" law doesn't affect crime rates. Ian Ayres and John Donahue, who wrote the most substantial critique of Lott's work, observe that "during the 1990s crime in non-shall-issue states fell far more than in shall-issue states." One of Lott's co-authors replied, weakly, that "must issue" laws in the 1990s were so different from earlier ones—fees were higher, training requirements were stiffer, and permit-holders were barred from carrying concealed weapons in more places such as churches—that they really shouldn't count as true "must issue" laws.

The differences between data from states that adopted "must issue" laws relatively early and those that did so later also seem to affect the robustness of Lott's results. Here too the idea is simple: Lott has many more "observations" from states that adopted early. If there's something that connects early adoption to reductions in crime rates, his analysis is going to be tilted in favor of showing such reductions, because more numbers from the early adopters are going to be in the mathematical model. When Ayres and Donahue tried to adjust for this effect, they found that adopting a "must issue" law didn't affect crime rates.

And indeed, there's at least a story that explains the connection between early adoption and reductions in crime rates. Early adopters seem to be states that began with relatively low crime rates, which experienced sharp increases in crime. Those increases generated political pressure to do something, which in turn led to the adoption of "must issue" laws. And then crime rates dropped, not because of the "must issue" laws but because the spike in crime rates went away and crime returned to its earlier, relatively low level.

Lott himself had made the point in his initial analysis: "Must issue" laws "have so far been adopted by relatively low-crime states in which the crime rate is rising." He tried to incorporate this in his analysis by using a different statistical technique. That technique involves finding some measure "that is correlated with the presence of a shall-issue law but uncorrelated with crime (except through the influence of the shall-issue law on crime)." Lott used these measures: rates for and changes in the rates of violent and property crime, percentage of state population in the National Rifle Association, percentage voting for the Republican presidential candidate, state racial composition, the size of the state population in absolute terms, and the region in which states were located. Donahue suggests that only NRA membership satisfies the requirements of the statistical technique Lott used: Crime rates clearly shouldn't be included, and armchair political analysis suggests that Republican presidential candidates are likely to get more votes when crime is rising. Ayres and Donahue reproduced Lott's results, and then excluded the crime rates from the analysis. They found that "when the flawed instruments are dropped . . . , the estimated effect on crime of shall-issue law adoption is never significantly different from zero."

There's a final problem with Lott's results when you take early adoption into account: They describe truly enormous reductions in crime rates. Homicides go down 67 percent, rapes 65 percent, and assaults 73 percent. Everything we know about the effects of policy interventions on crime rates suggests that these numbers are "implausibly high."

The National Academy of Sciences committee gave "more guns, less crime" "special attention." It found that some of Lott's results may have resulted from errors in the underlying data on which he relied. It also concluded that correcting the coding errors Ayres and Donahue identified yielded the results they reported, contrary to some earlier claims by Lott's co-authors. These were details, though. More important, the committee worked with Lott's own data, which he supplied the committee, to see if it could figure out why different scholars came to such different conclusions.

First, the committee replicated Lott's study by running the data he used in 1992 through Lott's own model, and came up with the same results. But the committee did more. Lott had compiled additional data for the years from 1993 to 1997. The committee took that larger set of numbers and, again, ran it through Lott's initial model. If his model was accurate—that is, if it identified all the things that affected crime rates, and could isolate the effects of adopting "must issue" laws—you ought to get pretty much the same results for the longer period as you do for the shorter one. What did the committee find? In one version, "[t]he re-sults...changed substantially." Adopting a must issue law did lead to a decrease in the murder rate, though a somewhat smaller one than Lott's initial study showed. But, strikingly, adopting such a law now appeared to *increase* overall crime rates and the rates for aggravated assault, robbery, property crime, car theft, burglary, and larceny. The increases for crimes in which the criminal doesn't expect to meet up with a victim, like car theft and burglary, might fit into Lott's overall theory of why more guns produce less of certain kinds of crime. The increases for assault and robbery, though, are quite puzzling. Why hadn't Lott himself come up with that revision? Because, when he used the expanded data set, he also changed his model, adding a number of new variables, such as state poverty and unemployment rates. The committee observed that "[t]hese seemingly minor adjustments cause substantial changes to the results."

The committee used the same data to examine another of Lott's approaches, which it called the "trend specification." Here Lott's model did somewhat better, showing decreases in crime rates across the board, although smaller ones than he had found for the period up to 1992. There was one problem, though. If you look at crime rates on a year-by-year basis, what happens? In the first five years after a "must issue" law is adopted, murder and property crime rates increase, and there are smaller decreases in rates for rape, assault, robbery, and overall crime. The effects of "must issue" laws seem to kick in six years after they are adopted: "One needs to include at least 6 years following the prelaw-change period to find statistically significant reductions in the violent crime and murder trends." Maybe it takes some time for criminals to figure out the new risks they face under a "must issue" law, which would explain why you don't observe effects until six years down the line, but it's quite hard to come up with an intuitively appealing story about why adopting a "must issue" law causes crime increases at first, then crime reductions several years later.

The committee observed that getting different results from pushing the larger and smaller data sets through the same model was "evidence of model misspecification" and suggested that "the estimated effects of right-to-carry laws are artifacts of specification errors." Its overall conclusion was this:

[I]n light of (a) the sensitivity of the empirical results to seemingly minor changes in model specification, (b) a lack of robustness of the results to the inclusion of more recent years of data . . . , and (c) the imprecision of some results, it is

impossible to draw strong conclusions from the existing literature on the causal impact of these laws.

One committee member, James Q. Wilson, dissented. A political scientist who made his reputation as a student of urban
politics, Wilson later turned to the study of urban police. In the
1980s, Wilson helped propound the "broken windows" theory of
urban crime: When potential criminals saw lots of broken windows in a neighborhood or got away with jumping the toll gates in
the subway system, they figured that the police weren't doing
much to maintain order and escalated their crimes to muggings
and worse. This theory led New York's police commissioner
William Bratton to adopt an aggressive version of "order maintenance" policing, which many conservatives believed was the
reason New York's crime rate declined substantially in the 1990s.
It probably wasn't—cities that continued to use traditional policing techniques had even larger reductions in crime rates in the
1990s—but it seemed like a neat idea.

So too was "more guns, less crime" for Wilson. Writing in 2000,
before the committee was appointed, Wilson wrote, "Lott's work
convinces me that the decrease in murder and robbery in states
with shall-issue laws ... is real and significant." His work on the
committee reduced Wilson's enthusiasm only a bit. He acknowledged that he couldn't be confident about the argument that more
guns meant less crime of all sorts, but he remained impressed that
nearly every way of massaging the data indicated that "must issue" laws led to reductions in the murder rate, and that neither he
nor the committee found enough evidence that such laws actually increased crime rates. So, he said, "the best evidence is that
[such laws] impose no costs but may confer benefits." Maybe
"must issue" laws were effective when crime rates were rising and
ineffective otherwise (although he didn't suggest that people

should be allowed to carry concealed weapons only during crime waves). Wilson opened his dissent by saying that he was "not an econometrician," and the committee responded by capitalizing on that admission, pointing out that Wilson's modest conclusions were inconsistent with what the econometric models really showed. "All of the studies...attempt to control for trends in crime.... If the effects vary by time, all of the existing models are misspecified"—which means that you can't rely on *any* of their results, including the results for murder.

What's the bottom line? Lott's critics occasionally suggest that more guns mean more crime, as criminals will respond to "must issue" laws by arming themselves even more heavily and shooting even more quickly. John Donahue observes that "the typical gun permit holder is a middle-aged Republican white male, which is a group at relatively low risk of violent criminal victimization." More guns in their hands might not mean less crime. Lott might reply, reasonably enough, that the point of adopting a "must issue" law would be to get more guns into the hands of African Americans, women, and Democrats. But all this seems to make too much of the evidence, which is basically a wash. Or, in the more academic terms used by the National Academy of Sciences committee, describing in identical terms works by two of Lott's collaborators and by two of his critics, "adoption of a right-to-carry law may increase, decrease, or have no discernible effect on the crime rate depending on the crime and the state that are involved."

There's more to the Lott story. An admirer describes John Lott as "a man of almost unparalleled intensity," with "something of a mad scientist about him." Lott sharply attacked the National Academy committee's report, writing, "all but one of its members (whose views on gun control were publicly known before their appointments) favored gun control." Sounds like fourteen of the committee's fifteen members went into the study supporting gun control, right? But watch those parentheses. In a book published in 2003, after the committee had been appointed but before it submitted its report, Lott identified four committee members as pro–gun control, including Steven Levitt. James Q. Wilson, the committee dissenter, was, Lott said, "the only member whose views were known in advance to not be entirely pro-gun control." So, what Lott said—and it might be accurate, albeit misleading—was that four of the five committee members whose views were known before their appointments were pro–gun control. He said nothing about the other ten members, but his column certainly leaves the impression that only Wilson was "not...entirely pro-gun control" going into the study.

Lott opened his book with a report of a survey he conducted. According to Lott, the survey showed that people who carried concealed weapons used them surprisingly often to deter criminal assaults: "98 per cent of the time that people use guns defensively, they merely have to brandish a weapon to break off an attack." Where did he get that figure? First he cited "national surveys" conducted by national polling organizations, but it turned out that none of the surveys actually had the 98 percent figure. Lott then referred to a survey he himself had conducted, polling 2,424 people. But, Lott said, his computer had crashed and he'd lost the data from the survey. Computer crashes do occur. Still, law professor and sociologist James Lindgren thought that there ought to be *some* evidence that the survey actually had been conducted—a research proposal, a grant awarding money for the survey, some research assistants who helped make the phone calls, *something*. But Lott couldn't provide Lindgren with anything at all: The phone calls had been made by undergraduate volunteers who worked for free and whose names Lott couldn't remember. Then Mary Rosh entered the scene. Lott, she wrote on websites, was a careful researcher and wonderful teacher. It turned out that Mary Rosh was what the blogosphere calls a "sock puppet"—John Lott himself, posting under a pseudonym.

What's interesting in all this is not whether Lott actually conducted the survey but that the questions raised about the survey cast a shadow over the rest of his argument, which relied on entirely different data and equations. In April 2006 Lott sued one of the authors of the best-selling book "Freakonomics" for defamation. In discussing Lott's arguments, Steven Levitt had written:

> Then there is the troubling allegation that Lott actually in-
> vented some of the survey data that support his more-guns/
> less-crime theory. Regardless of whether the data were faked,
> Lott's admittedly intriguing hypothesis doesn't seem to be
> true. When other scholars have tried to replicate his results,
> they found that right-to-carry laws simply don't bring down
> crime.

Lott didn't focus on the first sentence. Instead, he said that Levitt had defamed him by saying that other scholars couldn't "replicate" Lott's results. Why? For Lott, the term *replicate* has a precise meaning among economists: Take the very same data a study used, insert the numbers into the equations the study used, and see if the results are the same. It's true that nobody had failed to replicate Lott's results in that sense. As we've seen, the National Academy of Sciences did replicate Lott's results. But it's also true that other economists, using similar data and building similar equations, couldn't get the kinds of results Lott got. And some social scientists use the word "replicate" to describe *that* kind of research. Lott left the American Enterprise Institute a week before he filed the lawsuit—"abruptly," as one report put it. Defamation law runs up against free speech law, and there's basically no chance that Lott can win his lawsuit. In early 2007 a federal judge dismissed Lott's claim about "replication," but allowed the suit to go forward on another issue. The mere fact that Lott filed his lawsuit, no matter how unlikely success was, suggests that controversies seemingly about gun control and gun rights are actually about something else—not merely a person's reputation, but his position as a combatant in the culture wars.

Lott attracts, and takes part in, flame wars on the Internet. Some aspects of the flame wars aren't surprising: People who think that gun control is good policy disagree with Lott's conclusions; people who think otherwise agree with him. Scattered in the comments, though, you can occasionally find something particularly notable: People whose defense of the individual-rights view of the Second Amendment rests on their interpretation of the original understanding are persuaded by Lott's evidence. For a real originalist, that evidence would be completely irrelevant. Indeed, it wouldn't matter to a true originalist that Lott might have it exactly backward, and that more guns meant more crime. And, it would seem, there shouldn't be any connection between what you found in the historical sources and what you found in evidence about contemporary gun policies.

Why, then, do many originalist individual-rights proponents take Lott's side? Two possibilities:

- Even they recognize, with Justice Breyer, that constitutional interpretation takes consequences into account, and that their case would be weakened—as a *constitutional* argument—if Lott is dramatically wrong, and that it is strengthened if he is right.

- Positions on gun issues—whether about interpreting the Constitution or interpreting the data—depend not on the Constitution or the data but on something else, that is, where one stands in the culture wars.

The "culture wars" question arises repeatedly in discussions of gun policy. After examining two additional policy proposals to show the pattern, I'll turn to the culture wars.

"Safe storage" laws have become popular as a result of incidents like the shooting of Khalid Ali. Such laws make it a crime for a gun owner to keep weapons in places easily accessible to children. Florida adopted the first safe-storage law in 1989. Its law, emulated in more than a dozen states over the next decade, allows a gun's owner to be prosecuted if a child gets access to a gun and shoots himself or another person (covering suicides and accidents), or uses the gun to threaten someone else. Safe-storage laws sometimes specify that guns have to be kept in a locked box or have locks on their triggers.

The basic idea behind safe-storage laws is simple: If guns are locked up, kids can't get at them easily, and so they can't use them to commit suicide or, as in Khalid Ali's case, to shoot someone else accidentally. But, gun-rights advocates immediately point out, if guns are locked up, they can't easily be used to threaten a criminal who invades your home. And, they observe, enforcing safe-storage laws takes an odd form. The authorities only learn of "unsafe storage" after the event, that is, after a kid gets at a gun and uses it with disastrous outcomes. What, though, does the existence of a safe-storage law add to the prosecutors' armory? Norma Geil faced a bunch of criminal charges already. And, as the death of Khalid Ali suggests, the lives of people who violate safe-storage laws are likely to be so disorganized that making sure their guns are stored safely is low on the list of things you'd want to have them do to reduce the risk of violent death. The gain to Khalid Ali of effective enforcement of anti-drug laws, for example, would dwarf whatever benefit he might have gotten from the existence of a safe-storage law that the Geils are unlikely to have obeyed anyway. By and large, though with obvious exceptions, the people who comply with safe-storage laws aren't the same people whose children use guns to commit suicide or to show off at parties. Finally, in cases where unsafe storage leads to suicide, prosecutors and juries are going to feel the pull of the sentiment that the parents who didn't comply with the safe-storage law have suffered enough.

Again, it looks like we ought to be able to find out by looking at the facts whether safe-storage laws reduce gun violence. So, what do the studies show? John Lott and a colleague concluded that safe-storage laws don't have any real effect on juvenile suicide or gun accidents, but—no surprise here—that "the 15 states that had the safe-storage law in effect in 1996 experienced 3,758 more rapes, 26,724 more robberies, and 69,741 more burglaries," presumably because criminals were emboldened by the prospect that they could commit their crimes against gun owners who wouldn't be able to pull the guns out of storage fast enough to deter the crime. The precision of these numbers ought to lead us to raise our eyebrows: Exactly 3,757 more rapes, not 3,753 or 3,762? Perhaps the authors have become hyper-precise captives of their theory.

Another study comes to a rather different conclusion—again, no surprise. It too found no real effect of safe-storage laws on teen suicide using guns. But "[a]mong children younger than 15 years, unintentional shooting deaths were reduced by 23% (95% confidence interval, 6%–37%)." Why the difference in results? It's not entirely that Lott was measuring one thing—total crime—while the competing study measured only juvenile deaths, because Lott didn't find any effect on accidental shooting deaths. The NAS research council's committee observed, using terms we've heard before, "The formal models and specifications differ."

The committee was skeptical about both studies, which assumed that safe-storage laws "were the only notable event that might have affected firearms related injury and crime." Again, there's Florida: Florida's legislature had considered and rejected a safe-storage proposal shortly before it enacted the statute in 1989, after "a sharp increase in accidental injuries and fatalities." But suppose that increase was just a random spike, and the number of such injuries dropped back to its "normal" level over the next couple of years. The only thing in the models that changed was the adoption of the safe-storage law, so the models would tell us that adopting the law made a difference. But maybe it didn't; maybe the level of accidental injury was just floating back down to its normal level. And finally, the worst possibility of all: Maybe adopting the law changed the way the authorities described— "coded"—what had happened. "[I]f after the law is passed accidental shootings are more likely to be classified as suicides or homicides, then the observed empirical results may be due to coding changes rather than the law."

It would be nice to think that disagreements over policy could be resolved by empirical evidence. And maybe some can—but not, I think, policy disputes about which people care intensely. The reason is that all empirical studies are imperfect, as good social scientists admit. Partisans will identify real flaws—that is, flaws that social scientists would agree are defects—in studies that point to conclusions with which they disagree, and try to explain away the flaws their opponents identify in the studies that support the policies with which they agree. You pay your money and your make your choice among studies to believe—and you make your choice based on your overall orientation to the culture wars.

"Surely,... if the NRA and ATF [the federal Bureau of Alcohol, Tobacco, and Firearms] are advancing the same cause, there must be more here than meets the eye," wrote conservative law professor John Baker. The cause was Project Exile, an initiative by the United States Attorney in Richmond, Virginia, to ensure that everyone who used a gun to commit a crime would get five years added to his sentence, as federal law allowed. The NRA embraced Project Exile. So did candidate George W. Bush, who answered a question about gun control laws during one of the 2000 presidential debates, calling Project Exile "a great program." We should, Bush said, "enforce laws on the books." The NRA endorsed that approach as an *alternative* to enacting new gun-control laws, but enhanced enforcement of existing laws can stand alone as gun policy.

"Enforce the laws on the books" sounds like an obviously sensible policy that everyone should be able to endorse. Janet Reno's Department of Justice initiated Project Exile, and described it as one of the "Promising Strategies to Reduce Gun Violence" in a pamphlet it produced in 1999. In 1998, the Republican Policy Committee of the United States Senate criticized the Clinton administration for failing to provide adequate funds for expanding Project Exile, which it called "perhaps the most aggressive, innovative and creative crime control program ever initiated," and touted Senate Republican support for expanding it. Other conservatives, like Baker, weren't so sure. One gun-rights advocacy group, Gun Owners of America, denounced the program: "Instead of going after decent gun owners, state officials need to crack down on all violent criminals. Someone who kills with a knife is just as much a murderer as the one who kills with a gun."

Project Exile offers a good entry point into an examination of the "enforce the laws we have" policy. That policy sounds good at first, but on closer inspection things get more complicated. It turns out that Project Exile—and the "enforce the laws" policy—raises exactly the same problems of evidence and general policy that every other gun policy does. The NRA and ATF could support Project Exile because it was an example of what some legal scholars call "feel-good, do-something" programs, symbolizing bipartisan commitment to reducing gun violence without actually doing much.

Project Exile began when prosecutors in Richmond got upset at the city's extremely high homicide rate. They decided to go after criminals who used guns while committing their crimes and, perhaps more important, to go after people previously convicted of felonies who were barred from possessing guns. The project operated out of the U.S. Attorney's office, with cooperation from the state district attorney, who assigned a deputy to work with the federal prosecutors. When a Richmond police officer came across a gun while investigating a crime or interrogating a suspect, the officer paged an ATF agent, on call 24-7. The ATF consulted with the state and federal prosecutors to see if the person with the gun could be charged with some crime. If so, the prosecutors charged the defendant with the crime, whether state or federal, that carried the highest potential sentence. Previously convicted felons and drug offenders who used guns typically were charged with federal crimes, violent felons who used guns with state ones. Charging a federal crime also had the advantage of allowing pretrial detention without bail in more circumstances—and, giving the project its name, the likelihood that the defendant would be exiled to serve his sentence in a federal prison far away from Richmond.

Supporters of Project Exile touted its apparent success: In a year and a half, nearly 400 people were charged with federal crimes, 300 held by the state, over 200 held without bond, almost 250 defendants convicted, with sentences averaging four-and-a-half years, and 440 guns seized. Of course these are what might be called input measures, showing who Project Exile caught rather than whether the project reduced gun violence. But it seemed that it did: Richmond's homicide rate declined by 33 percent between 1997, when Project Exile started, and 1998.

Social programs that successful are rare, and not surprisingly Project Exile produced its share of critics. Some of the criticisms were pretty theoretical, others rather trivial, but one was substantial.

Project Exile swept a lot of cases into the federal criminal system, just when the Supreme Court and others were expressing unease about the "overfederalization" of crime: If Richmond wanted to reduce its homicide rate, it should enforce *state* law more vigorously, not transfer authority to the federal government. Many conservatives signed on to the *general* "overfederalization" criticism. But ordinary people tend not to worry about the theory of federalism; they care about gun violence and homicides.

Federal judges weighed in on Project Exile as well. One wrote Chief Justice William Rehnquist that Project Exile had turned the federal court in Richmond "into a minor-grade police court"— a point that ordinary citizens might well think elitist. Joined by two others, the same judge, while upholding Project Exile's constitutionality, tweaked its supporters by pointing out that most of those serving federal sentences did so in Petersburg, Virginia, twenty-five miles away—hardly an exile from Richmond.

Others came up with more substantial criticisms. In 2001 *US News and World Report* examined Project Exile after four years. The number of indictments dropped each year, declining from 254 to 140; conviction rates declined by about the same amount, and pre-trial detention, while still common, was occurring less frequently. Sentences ranged from one year up, showing that somewhere someone—defense lawyers, prosecutors, or judges—wasn't really committed to the project's broadest aspirations. Prodded by the success of the federal program, Virginia created its own, which absorbed many cases from the federal system. But the Virginia program didn't work nearly as well. The conviction rate was a strikingly low 40 percent. A Richmond prosecutor said that it was his job "to drop cases that are not prosecutable," while federal prosecutors, with greater resources, could pursue every case that fell within Project Exile's guidelines. According to the story, "A private coalition that raised nearly $500,000 to promote federal and state Exile programs suspended funding for its advertising campaign this year, citing Virginia Exile's lousy performance."

Even inputs weren't doing so well. What about outputs? Steven Raphael and Jens Ludwig, two social scientists, looked at outputs—the Richmond homicide rate. They showed that Richmond, like many other cities, had experienced a large increase in the murder rate in the 1980s and early 1990s, and that Richmond, like other cities, then experienced a large decline in those rates. Richmond did better after Project Exile, but only because it had done a lot worse before it. Basically, Raphael and Ludwig noted a spike in homicide rates everywhere—larger in Richmond than elsewhere—and then a return to a more "normal" murder rate. Their reason: the crack epidemic, whose growth caused the spike in homicides and whose decline returned the homicide rate to its "normal" level. Evaluations based solely on a decrease from 1997 were misleading, they argued, because the murder rate deviated from its long-term decline *only* in 1997. Project Exile had some effect on the declining murder rate—"approximately 6 homicides per 100,000 residents, or 15 percent." Prosecutors could have increased sentences for traffic violations and claimed that doing so led to a reduction in the murder rate. Or, as Raphael and Ludwig put it more delicately, "almost all of the observed decrease probably would have occurred even in the absence of the program."

Of course a 15 percent reduction in the homicide rate is nothing to sneeze at. Still, there might be more effective ways of getting there. Indeed, Project Exile was only one of sixty programs the Department of Justice identified in its report. Many of the others, though, didn't have Project Exile's political attractions. Conservatives were likely to deride some as merely social work—a program to teach gun safety, a program that "brings together police officers and mental health professionals for mutual training, consultation, and support so that they may effectively provide direct interdisciplinary intervention to children and families who are victims, witnesses, or perpetrators of violent crimes." These programs might reduce gun violence in the long run, but no politician is going to get much credit for supporting them from those worried about gun violence on the streets today and tomorrow.

Other programs involved intensive police patrolling in a Kansas City neighborhood with a high homicide rate and "saturation patrols" in high-crime areas of Milwaukee. These programs fit well into the "enforce the laws we have" approach, but they have many drawbacks. Stopping any car for *any* motor vehicle violation or only ones that were "suspicious" because they fit a profile might be constitutional under Supreme Court precedents, but they do raise civil liberties issues and, perhaps more important, have ambiguous effects on affected communities (mostly minority, of course): Some community members welcome the police and their "intrusions" on privacy because they fear criminals more; others resent the police disruption of their law-abiding lives.

Intensive police patrols are also expensive. Even Project Exile, which turned out to be relatively cheap, lost financial support. A Seattle program aimed at aggressive enforcement of gun laws against juvenile offenders increased conviction rates and sentences; it ended when a grant providing funds for the prosecutor's position dedicated to the program ran out.

"Enforce the laws we have" is a good slogan, but it ignores budgets. After all, why haven't prosecutors and police *already* decided to enforce the laws we already have? The experience with Virginia Exile suggests the answer: They have more important crimes to investigate and prosecute. Money to support enforcing gun laws has to come from somewhere. And generally that means reducing funding for some other law enforcement initiatives. We have to think about the *politics* of Project Exile and similar initiatives, and here we return to the alliance between the NRA and ATF: Project Exile was a really neat way for ATF to begin to rebuild its reputation in the gun-rights community after the disaster it had experienced in the Branch Davidian raid in Waco, Texas. (If *you* aren't familiar with the details of that raid, no matter: The gun-rights community is.) ATF could go after street violence and pay less attention to what gun-control proponents call "rogue" gun dealers, who have some support in the gun-rights community because the laws they break (if they do) aren't laws that we *should* have, as gun-rights proponents see things.

The "enforce the laws we already have" slogan overlooks something else—what social scientists call the "migration" of crime. Enforce the laws we already have in Richmond, and criminals go to the suburbs, outside the scope of the program. We saw this in connection with local bans on gun sales: Tell gun dealers that they can't open a store in your town, and they'll set up shop a few miles down the road. When Oakland adopted ordinances aimed at making life hard for gun dealers, the number in the city dropped from 115 to seven within a year, but we have no idea whether the 100 dealers driven out of Oakland went out of business or simply relocated—although I know which way I'd bet.

Law breakers migrate too. Kansas City intensified police patrols in an eighty-block "hotspot" area. Among the results: "Drive-by shootings dropped from 7 to 1 in the target area, while increasing from 6 to 12 in a comparison area." Unless the police have the resources to patrol intensively everywhere, it's hard to see what this intervention accomplished. When police stopped every car with a motor vehicle violation in one Indianapolis neighborhood, violent crimes *increased*. Why? The evaluators suggested, "Because directed patrols had been used for 2 years . . . , adaptive behavior by violators may explain this increase." Or, dropping the jargon, criminals figured out that they ought to keep their cars in good repair and drive carefully.

The Department of Justice under Janet Reno offered a full menu of promising programs to reduce gun violence. It seemed, though, to want to ensure that public policy was "healthy," using different varieties—law enforcement *and* social work. Its support for Project Exile was regularly coupled with praise for Boston's comprehensive approach. Law professor Daniel Richman captured the department's position in a phrase: "Let a thousand flowers bloom, but Boston may well be better."

Boston had many program elements, combining law enforcement with social work. In "Operation Ceasefire," directed at gang violence, probation and police officers went to gang members and told them that "there would be swift, sure, and severe consequences for violence." Talking with gang members, officers said, "We're here because of the shooting. We're not going to leave until it stops. And until it does, nobody is going to so much as jaywalk, nor make any money, nor have any fun." The "Boston Gun Project" inspected gun dealers and, in the end, led sixty-five to go out of business (or go elsewhere, or go underground), with only seventeen gun dealers remaining in the city. "Operation Night Light" involved surprise nighttime visits by probation officers to find out whether those under supervision were violating the terms of their probation by associating with gang members. The social work elements involved connecting young men to social services, job training, and "conflict-resolution training."

And did it work? One analysis indicated that Operation Ceasefire, at least, wasn't any better than Project Exile—and that Project Exile was better than Raphael and Ludwig thought, with perhaps a 20 percent reduction in the homicide rate. Or maybe not: "The Richmond results inspire somewhat greater confidence in the existence of a difference between Richmond's firearm homicide trend and the average trend..., although the difference may have been quite small."

Steven Levitt, the target of John Lott's defamation suit, argues that most of the conventional reasons given for the decline in crime in the 1990s—the end of the crack epidemic, the strong economy, increased numbers of police on the streets—actually explain only a small amount of the decline, and that the real reason was legalized abortion, which, a decade and a half earlier, had allowed many women whose children would have grown up to be criminals to have abortions instead. Levitt's controversial theory aside, it seems reasonably clear that we shouldn't put too much faith in specific strategies like Project Exile as crime-reduction programs.

Raphael and Ludwig conclude their evaluation of Project Exile with this: "[I]t may be worthwhile to implement interventions that have quite modest effects on gun violence." That may be the most we can say about what *any* gun policy will accomplish: It will have quite modest effects—perhaps to reduce gun violence or crime a bit, perhaps to increase them a bit.

Take the licensing-test proposal. Nearly everyone who takes it will pass, if not at first then on a second or third try. And maybe studying for the test will make people a little more careful in how they handle guns once they get them. In working on this book I decided to take a sample online test offered by a commercial test preparation service for the Canadian firearms safety test. I have general test-taking skills, but I have never fired or even handled a gun (not for any ideological reason—it just never seemed like a valuable use of my time). Without doing any studying at all and relying only on my general knowledge about weapons, I got a score of 68 percent. How? If you read the newspapers, you know that there's something called a "hollow-point" bullet, and that such bullets are really bad. So when the test shows some ammunition with a deep depression at the point and asks whether "The ammunition pictured for this revolver can be legally imported into Canada," it's a pretty good guess that they are showing you hollow-point bullets, and that the answer is "No." Another question was, "In ACTS & PROVE, the 'C' stands for" what? I had no idea what ACTS & PROVE is, but when the choices the text gives are these—cartridges stay out until you are ready to shoot, control the muzzle direction, crime is created by unregistered firearms, or cover the muzzle to keep out debris—again it is not hard to figure out that because this is a test on knowledge about firearms safety the "crime" answer is probably wrong, and because ACTS & PROVE is obviously a short-hand memory device, the "cartridges" answer is probably wrong because it is too long. That leaves a choice between the two "muzzle" answers, and the one referring to debris seems likely to involve an uncommon situation. So, the sensible answer is "control the muzzle direction."

(I checked later, and ACTS & PROVE stands for Assume every firearm is loaded; Control the muzzle direction at all times; Trigger finger must be kept off the trigger and out of the trigger guard; See that the firearm is unloaded—PROVE it safe; Point the firearm in the safest available direction; Remove all cartridges; Observe the chamber; Verify the feeding path; Examine the bore.)

As it happens, my 68 percent means I would not have passed the real test, which requires an 80 percent score. But I am sure that by studying even a tiny bit I could have gotten the five additional correct answers that would have given me a passing score. And yet I would not say that I would be any more likely to use a gun safely after passing the test than before.

Even more, we worry about gun safety in real-world situations, not in the artificial setting of a licensing test, even the "practical" part where you have to demonstrate your ability to handle guns safely. True, it may make some difference that you "instantly fail the exam" if you point your gun at a human being while you are taking the test. But often the whole point of having a gun is that you *can* point it at a human being—the person who is threatening you. And when that happens, you are likely to be under stress, fearful, and far less likely to remember all the "rules" about gun use you learned. Gun use is different from driving because drivers get a lot of experience in using the roads safely, even in unsafe conditions like snow and ice, but gun users rarely use their guns in the stressful circumstances where we rightly worry about the possibility of unsafe use.

That the effects seem likely to be small can't account for the intensity of the debates over gun policy, though. As one comment on Raphael and Ludwig's work put it, "Why does scientific evidence carry so little weight in this field?" The reason is the culture wars, which manifest themselves here through "slippery slope" arguments: Adopt a licensing test, and the next thing you know, gun owners will be required to register their guns; after gun registration comes confiscation. Logicians know that slippery-slope arguments are quite tricky. The problem with them is this: At the time a particular policy is put forward, the proponent says, "This is a good policy, but I understand that there are good reasons for stopping here." Why would the good reasons disappear once the policy is in place? That is, why would we slide down the slippery slope if we think that there are good reasons to stop at the first step? The answer is something like this: The very fact that we have adopted and lived with the initial policy will lead us to think later on that there are no good reasons counseling against taking the second step—from passing a test to registration, from registration to confiscation.

Exactly how that would happen in the context of gun policy is unclear. One candidate explanation is that proponents of more extensive gun control would be able to portray the licensing test as a successful policy intervention, one that made people's lives a little safer. So, they will argue—and some who might have been skeptical or neutral at first might agree—why not take the second step, to registration, and make us even more safe? Gun-rights proponents might contest the claim that the licensing test made much difference, but, as I read the literature, they are more likely to claim that the improvement in safety is not worth it and, more important, that the desire for small increases in safety is symptomatic of an unattractive character trait that has unfortunately become widespread in the contemporary United States.

Here too we need to think about the culture wars. Not the "red-state/blue-state" culture wars, though. It's easy enough to understand why people who support gun control believe that the social scientific evidence establishes that requiring "safe storage" increases safety overall, taking into account accidents prevented and crimes undeterred, and why gun-rights supporters believe that the social scientific evidence supports the "more guns, less crime" theory. But there's no obvious reason why a person who regularly goes to church—a "red state" voter—would be more likely to support gun rights than gun control, or why a person who doesn't believe in God—a "blue state" voter—would be more likely to support gun control. Indeed, it's easy to spell out a hypothesis that atheists would be gun-rights proponents: They think that, there being no higher power, we are on our own and can rely only on ourselves to survive. (Think Ayn Rand here.)

Some social scientists have developed a "cultural theory of risk" that tries to explain why people disagree over what would seem to be straightforward factual matters. The basic idea is simple: If you believe that some activities are good or honorable, you're likely to believe factual assertions that can be taken to make it "sensible" for people to engage in those activities. Dan Kahan and Donald Braman, who apply the cultural theory of risk to gun policy, give this example: "[A] person may climb mountains on the weekends to demonstrate...that she possesses courage and self-discipline" and "it is easy to believe that ignoble activities are also physically dangerous, and worthy ones benign." So, our mountain-climber is not likely to find credible any social scientific research "showing" that mountain-climbing isn't all that dangerous and will discount criticisms of that research for failing to take some variables into account. In the context of gun policy: What's the first image that flashes into your mind when you think about guns? Natty Bumppo (probably not, but you get the idea) or John F. Kennedy, John Wayne or Martin Luther King, Jr.? If the first of these pairs, you're likely to think that John Lott's study was a good one; if the second, that his critics are correct.

According to the cultural theory of risk, "Common values lead to common fears.... We choose the risks [to worry about] in the same package as we choose our social institutions." And those choices are driven by a larger package of value orientations. The jargon of the cultural theory of risk identifies three packages: hierarchical, egalitarian, and individualist. The labels are pretty descriptive. People with a hierarchical view "favor social conservatism" and like "traditional forms of social and political authority." Egalitarians "favor[] collective action to equalize wealth, status, and power." And "the individualist view prizes individual autonomy, celebrates free markets and other institutionalized forms of private ordering, and resents collective interference with" them. The payoff from these seemingly banal descriptions is this: The view you have—individualist, hierarchical, egalitarian—makes you more alert to some risks, less alert to others. And the view you have also leads you to accept evidence that confirms your view more readily than you will accept evidence in tension with it, and to trust people who share your views more than you trust people who disagree.

Kahan and Braman used the cultural theory of risk to explain differing attitudes on gun policy. They began with the obvious "red state/blue state" observations: Whites, Protestants, men, and people who live in rural areas are substantially more likely to oppose gun control than African Americans, Catholics and Jews, women, and people who live in cities. They looked at a large-scale attitude survey, sorting people into the three cultural orientations based on their views about capital punishment, gays, the military, and welfare programs—but not gun policy. Once people were sorted into the groups, Kahan and Braman examined their views on gun policy. They found that "the more egalitarian... an individual's worldview, the more likely that person was to support gun control" and "the more hierarchical and individualistic the respondent's worldview, the more likely she was to oppose gun control." These differences were *big*: two to four times greater support for gun control depending on what your cultural orientation is. And confirming that the "red state/blue state" account isn't enough, the differences based on cultural orientations were larger than differences based on anything else, like race or religion—and larger than differences based on party affiliation or identification as a conservative or liberal. So, as Kahan and Braman put it, we can't reduce disagreements on gun policy to "conventional political ideologies." Something else—cultural orientation—is at work: "[A]fter cultural orientations are controlled for, whether one is black, resides in the South, resides in the Northeast, or lives in an urban area... no longer have *any* significant effect." Another study looked at beliefs about facts, and found that people with "hierarchical and individualistic orientations saw guns as substantially... safer than did those [with] egalitarian" orientations.

Putting all this together, Kahan and Braman conclude:

> [T]hose involved in the gun control debate aren't really arguing about whose perception of risk is more grounded in empirical reality; they are arguing about what it would *say* about our shared values to credit one or the other side's fears through law. For the... opponents of gun control, it would be a cowardly and dishonorable concession to our own physical weaknesses for us to disarm all private citizens in the interest of public safety. For the proponent of gun control, it would send an unacceptable message of mutual distrust in each

other's intentions, of collective indifference to each other's welfare...to rely on each citizen's decision to arm herself as a means of keeping the civil peace.

The cultural theory might make us pretty depressed about the possibility of coming up with a sensible gun policy—whether the policy favors gun rights or gun control—because we as a society might not really be concerned about good policy. In Kahan and Braman's words, "the lesson of the recent outpouring of high-quality empirical studies is neither 'more guns, less crime' nor 'more guns, more crime,' but rather 'more statistics, less persuasion.'"

Of course, the cultural theory of risk is a social scientific theory, and the evidence offered to support it is subject to the standard "the specification of the model is incorrect" criticism. So, for example, two skeptics about the theory worry that it can't explain why "over half of those who support moderate controls oppose a ban on the private ownership of handguns." And even more, if the cultural theory of risk is right, or even close to right, people will find it plausible or not depending on their cultural orientations. The same two critics, themselves social scientists, make the point by noting "the irony of...using multivariate regression analysis as a tool of persuasion to argue that multivariate regression analyses are not persuasive." Which suggests another reason that social science is not going to give us a way to resolve disagreements over gun policy.

The cultural theory of risk sheds light not just on debates over gun policy but also on debates over the Second Amendment's meaning. We've seen that, on originalist grounds, the gun-rights interpretation is a bit stronger than the gun-control interpretation, but that the gun-control interpretation is stronger when you take into account all the methods courts use to interpret constitutional provisions.

But suppose somehow we confined ourselves to the originalist interpretation. What difference would that make in the regulations governments could implement? No surprise here: The division between gun-rights advocates and gun-control advocates would simply be reproduced in this new setting. Recall here the minority report of the Pennsylvania ratification convention, which plays an important part in the originalist defense of the individual-rights position. After saying that "the people have the right to bear arms" and "no law shall be passed for disarming the people or any of them"—pretty clearly an individual-rights position—the report continued, "unless for crimes committed, or real danger of public injury from individuals." It's not hard to see how nearly every gun-control regulation could be justified as aiming to prevent "real danger of public injury from individuals." Of course, gun-rights proponents would demand much higher proof of "danger" than gun-control proponents. And equally obviously, gun-control proponents would prefer not to engage in a second level of analysis. Still, the "unless" clause shows how gun-control proponents might not find it any more difficult to defend the regulations they favor if they accepted the Standard Model—which, again, indicates that the disputes over the Standard Model are not really about why anyone interested in gun control or gun rights should care about it.

Consider the case of Timothy Joe Emerson. He and his wife Sacha were getting divorced. At a hearing in September 1998 to sort out their finances, Mrs. Emerson told the judge that Dr. Emerson had threatened to kill her lover. The judge issued an order barring Dr. Emerson from threatening her, their child, or anyone else. In November Mrs. Emerson went to Dr. Emerson's office to pick up a support check. They got into a verbal fight, and he got a pistol from his desk, pointed it at her and their child, and demanded that they leave the office. Two weeks later, in a conversation with police officers about an unrelated matter, Dr. Emerson told them that he had an AK-47 as well as other guns. According to the police officers, Dr. Emerson "said something about shooting his wife and her new boyfriend," and that any of his wife's friends who "set foot on his property" would "be found dead in the parking lot." A little over a week later, a federal grand jury indicted Dr. Emerson for the unlawful possession of the pistol he had used to threaten his wife in his office. The federal criminal law he was charged with violating says that anyone subject to a court order restraining him from "harassing, striking, or threatening an intimate partner... or child," cannot possess a gun. Dr. Emerson did indeed have several guns, all of them purchased legally when he acquired them—and, in fact, possessed legally up to the moment the judge issued the restraining order.

Dr. Emerson argued that the Second Amendment guaranteed an individual right to bear arms. The trial court and the court of appeals that considered his case agreed. Did that agreement help him? Hardly: The court of appeals held that the individual right to bear arms was subject to reasonable regulation, and that the "order of protection" provision was reasonable. After a trial, Dr. Emerson was sentenced to thirty months in federal prison.

Dr. Emerson's case shows that winning the battle over the individual-rights theory doesn't mean winning the war. The reason is that it's not enough to discover an individual right in the Constitution. Everyone agrees that legislatures have the power—sometimes—to regulate the exercise of individual rights. What does it take to justify such a regulation? Constitutional law recognizes two kinds of individual rights. Gun-rights advocates want the right to bear arms to be treated like the right to free speech—

something that the government can regulate only when there are really strong reasons for doing so. To use the Pennsylvania minority report's "unless" clause as an example of a criterion for justifying regulation: Proponents of gun rights would treat the "real danger" criterion as a serious limitation on government power. So, for example, they might require proof that a gun-control measure would actually reduce danger to the public. Gun-control advocates counter that the right to bear arms is like the right to own a car or a house—something the government can regulate easily and extensively. For them, the "real danger" criterion would be satisfied if a legislature could reasonably believe that a gun-control measure would reduce danger to the public.

Of course, accepting the Standard Model does imply that *some* gun-control regulations are unconstitutional, while rejecting it implies that almost none are. The unconstitutional ones would be at the core of the amendment's concerns, from the Standard Model's perspective. What might they be? As I've indicated, one would be a national ban on possessing guns. That is basically what the court of appeals held in the 2007 case involving the District of Columbia's ban on handgun possession. (The only peculiarity there is that the Second Amendment applied directly—not via "incorporation"—because the District is a federal enclave whose laws flow directly from the exercise of the national government's power to "exercise exclusive Legislation" of the District.) The only other real candidate for a core prohibition, I think, would be some statutes that deny some people access to guns while others are allowed to have them. But, as Dr. Emerson's case illustrates, exactly what this aspect of the Second Amendment might bar the government from doing is not at all obvious.

His case exemplifies one common gun-control strategy: Deny access to guns to some people because of what they have done: Dr. Emerson had threatened his ex-wife, others have committed felonies and served time. What about other selective denials of access to guns? The post–Civil War statutes barring African Americans from owning guns are clearly unconstitutional—not because of the Second Amendment, though, but because of the general prohibition on race discrimination in the Fourteenth Amendment's clause barring states from denying anyone the "equal protection of the laws." And it's actually quite hard to come up with examples of selective prohibitions that might be unconstitutional but that wouldn't be caught by the Equal Protection Clause. Gun-rights proponents might read into the Second Amendment some sort of concern for equal access to weapons, but it doesn't seem necessary to do so.

Gun-rights proponents agree that some of these prohibitions are clearly consistent with their view of the Second Amendment because, they say, such selective denials satisfy the high standard of justification they think the amendment requires. Taking guns away from law-abiding citizens, though, would be unconstitutional. During the crisis in New Orleans after Hurricane Katrina, law enforcement officials heard stories that some of those stranded in the city had shot at looters and, more important from the law enforcement point of view, at police officers. They responded by confiscating guns they found in the city's houses. Gun-rights proponents argued that the confiscations were at least foolish because they deprived vulnerable victims of defenses against marauders, probably illegal under state law, and perhaps unconstitutional. Congress responded by enacting a ban on confiscating guns during emergencies. Symptomatic of culture-wars legislation, this statute is almost entirely symbolic: Emergencies are, by definition, unusual, and gun confiscations during them even more so. Maybe this ban will prevent some looting as looters fear being shot by home owners; maybe it will cause some mistaken shootings of law enforcement officials trying to move fearful (and armed) people out of danger. Its effects, whatever they are, are surely going to be small. And this is as close to a problem with gun confiscation as we've recently gotten.

A "strong" Second Amendment built on the Standard Model might yield protections as strong as those afforded speech. Or it might yield protections that are strong along some dimensions but weaker along others. Whether it did, though, would depend on whether gun-rights or gun-control proponents won the *next* battle in the culture wars—the one that would take place after gun-control proponents stopped fighting the Standard Model (which, I should emphasize, they haven't done yet).

Because the courts haven't done much work with the individual-rights theory of the Second Amendment, just about the only decisions we have analyzing the government's power to regulate the individual right to bear arms are the appellate courts' decisions in Dr. Emerson's case and in the District of Columbia case. Because the latter involved a comprehensive ban, the decision said little about the scope of the power to regulate the individual right to keep and bear arms. In the former, the majority struggled to uphold the regulation, saying that the order of protection was "minimally" sufficient to justify the prosecution, or, in another version, that the connection between the restraining order and the risk of gun violence was "barely" enough.

The court *said* that "limited, narrowly tailored" restrictions were constitutional. That's the language courts use when they're dealing with "fundamental" rights like free speech. But if you look at what bothered the court, you can see why it came really close to treating the individual right to bear arms like the right to own a car. Dr. Emerson said that maybe his rights could be restricted if the divorce court had found that he really was a threat to his former wife or their child, but the court never made such a finding. The federal court thought that something like a finding about a threat had to be implicit in the divorce court's order, relying on Texas cases dealing with *other* kinds of restraining orders, but Dr. Emerson pointed out that under state law, he didn't have a right to appeal the restraining order, nor any way to find out whether any courts really thought that he posed a threat. Advocates for divorced men complain that judges in divorce courts issue restraining orders routinely, without giving any real attention to the particular facts of the case. Dr. Emerson made the same complaint, and the federal court upheld the restriction on his rights without any assurance that he was wrong. That's what courts do when they uphold restrictions on "ordinary" rights like the right to own your own car.

Gun-rights proponents might accept the Emerson decision as combining an enormous victory—the acknowledgment that the Second Amendment protects an individual right—accompanied by a temporary defeat. The Supreme Court's earliest decisions applying the First Amendment to political speech also upheld convictions, but they planted the seeds for later developments that have produced a set of free speech rules that make it really hard to convict someone for what he said. In the long run the Emerson decision might be seen as the first step in a longer path to substantial protections of gun rights. The District of Columbia decision would then be the second step.

Maybe not, though. The Second Amendment is the *national* Constitution's treatment of the right to keep and bear arms. More than forty states have provisions in their state constitutions protecting an individual right to bear arms. These provisions can't sensibly be interpreted to deal with militias, and state courts haven't tried. And yet, nearly every case interpreting these state constitutional provisions holds that state legislatures can regulate the right to keep and bear arms, as guaranteed by the state constitutions, by *reasonable* regulations—the weak standard rather than the strong one.

Against challenges based on these state constitutional provisions, which—again—clearly protect an individual right to keep and bear arms, state courts have upheld licensing laws, laws prohibiting carrying concealed weapons, and carrying loaded weapons, and complete bans on the possession of assault weapons anywhere in the state and even bans on the possession of handguns in specific cities. Indeed, it's hard to identify a gun-control policy that has *not* been upheld against challenges based on state constitutional guarantees of an individual right to keep and bear arms. We've seen that many of these policies might not be terribly effective in controlling violence. But, as a matter of law, state courts using an individual-rights approach to guarantees of the right to keep and bear arms have given legislatures about as wide a range of policy choice as they would have even if the state constitutions didn't protect the right. It turns out that gun-control proponents get a lot of what they want even in the face of these state constitutional rules—and so might get a lot of what they want were the federal courts to accept the Standard Model's interpretation of the Second Amendment.

To be sure, scattered state supreme court decisions apply a more stringent standard. Gun-rights proponents hope that decisions like *Emerson* might give those state court decisions greater prominence, so that they would become the thin end of a wedge that will eventually produce a more robust individual right to keep and bear arms. Gun-control proponents, in contrast, treat the cases as isolated ones, whose outcomes might have been shaped by the case's specific facts. In 2003, for example, the Wisconsin Supreme Court reversed a conviction for possessing a concealed weapon. Munir Hamdan ran a grocery and liquor store in a high-crime area of Milwaukee. The store had been robbed four times between 1993 and 1999. In 1997 Hamdan killed an armed robber in self-defense, and there was another fatal shooting in the store in 1999. Hamdan had also had a gun held to his head and survived only because the gun failed to fire when the trigger was pulled. He kept a handgun in the store and was charged with possessing a concealed weapon.

Hamdan thought he had a good constitutional defense. In 1998, the Wisconsin Constitution was amended to include this provision: "The people have the right to keep and bear arms for security, defense, hunting, recreation or any other lawful purpose." Hamdan lost in the lower courts, although it's worth noting that his sentence was a one dollar fine. The Wisconsin Supreme Court reversed Hamdan's conviction because prosecuting him for having a concealed weapon amounted to "practically nullifying the right" to self-defense. But in a case decided on the same day, it upheld the overall ban on carrying concealed weapons against a general constitutional challenge based on the new state constitutional provision. All the provision required was that legislatures adopt "reasonable" regulations. Applying the general prohibition in Hamdan's circumstances was unreasonable.

There's one final point. The Standard Model treats the Second Amendment's preamble as explaining the individual right, not placing conditions on it. Some gun-rights proponents let the preamble in by the back door, treating its reference to a "well regulated militia" as making it clear that legislatures can indeed regulate the right to keep and bear arms, and do so in ways that might not be allowed were other rights, lacking similar preambles, at stake. We know, for example, that the First Amendment prohibits the government from requiring you to get a license before you print a pamphlet, but maybe the Second Amendment allows licensing as a form of good regulation.

According to Saul Cornell, the citizen-oriented individual-rights approach actually *requires* a substantial amount of regulation. Under that approach, citizens have a duty to participate in the militia. But in performing that duty, they have to know how to use the guns they have. Elbridge Gerry of Massachusetts (later to become famous for inventing gerrymandering) wanted the Second Amendment to refer to "a well regulated militia, trained to arms." According to the Virginia ratifying convention, the well-regulated militia was "composed of the body of the people trained to arms." And who is to ensure that the training is adequate other than the government? Not only licensing but training might be required of anyone who owns a gun. Or, put another way, the government in pursuit of creating a well-regulated militia might prohibit anyone who hasn't received appropriate training from owning a gun. Governments that allow widespread gun ownership by people who can't use them correctly are, in this view, just as defective as governments that fail to protect us against private violence—and, indeed, their failure to regulate the citizen militia might *cause* that violence.

Taken on its own terms, the Emerson decision might have some straightforward implications even today. Perhaps a watered-down individual right to bear arms means that cities and states can't adopt complete bans on gun possession within their limits, as the court held in the District of Columbia case, although a couple of state court decisions uphold even such bans. Yet even that conclusion follows only if constitutional analysis begins and ends with the originalism that animates the Standard Model. But it doesn't. And the other components of competent constitutional analysis point pretty strongly in favor of a Second Amendment doctrine that would either reject the individual-rights interpretation or would allow such substantial government regulation of the right to bear arms that it wouldn't make any difference whether we accept or reject the Standard Model.

We can now come back to the licensing-test proposal for the last time. Is a licensing test a "limited and tailored" regulation of the individual right recognized in the Emerson case? A reasonable regulation of the right under the state courts' rules? As always, the answer is "Yes and no." As applied in the Emerson case, the constitutional standard is not demanding. Gun-control proponents would certainly say that a licensing test screens out at least a handful of people who would not use their guns safely, and that preparing for the test would teach people how to use their guns. Advocates of gun rights would respond that the "fit" between passing or failing a test and reducing unlawful gun use is extremely loose. As my experiment with the Canadian test suggests, lots of people who pass the test will not know much about guns (but may be good at taking tests), and the practical part of the test—shooting at a gun range, for example—does not reproduce the circumstances under which worrisome gun violence takes place. For gun-rights proponents, a licensing test is almost completely pointless—except as an expression of a cultural hostility to gun use entirely.

At every point, then—whether we are concerned with the basic choice between the Standard Model and more traditional interpretations of the Second Amendment, with the implications of the Standard Model, or with gun policy—the disagreements that the cultural theory of risk identifies simply reproduce themselves. Is there anything we can do? The Conclusion suggests some modest possibilities.

Conclusion

. . .

Usually no one "wins" battles in the culture wars. At best the combatants get tired and move on to some other confrontation. Could the culture war over the Second Amendment be different?

Polls suggest a couple of possibilities, though the polls have to be read with care. I emphasize first two groups of results, then add a third.

• Gun-control proponents take heart from findings, consistent for more than a decade and across different ways of asking the question, that a majority—once or twice a narrow majority, more often a quite substantial one—feels that the nation's gun laws should be made more strict. Typically, large majorities also say that they would like to see a bunch of specific new policies adopted, although I'd be more cautious about these responses. An example: In 1999–2000, between 70 percent and 75 percent of the subjects polled favored a national law requiring that all gun owners obtain licenses.

• Gun-rights proponents take heart from equally consistent findings that roughly similar majorities oppose the adoption of laws banning handgun possession. And on the Second Amendment itself, a poll in 2002 by ABC News found 73 percent of the subjects agreeing with the proposition that the Second Amendment guaranteed an individual right to own guns, and only 20 percent thinking that the Amendment referred only to state militias.

Unsophisticated gun-control proponents might see an easy out for them in these poll results. They could announce that they agree with the proposition that the Second Amendment protects an individual right to own guns, and then advocate gun-control policies other than a national ban on handgun possession. They could, for example, accept the underlying holding about the individual right to keep and bear arms in the District of Columbia case. But they need not accept that decision's bottom line, because they might even make an argument based on localism that individual cities and states might face special circumstances that would justify *local* bans on handgun possession—although, as we've seen, leakage of guns bought elsewhere into cities with complete bans makes the bans questionable on policy grounds—but point out that that allowing local bans doesn't mean that the Second Amendment allows a nationwide ban. Law professor Dan Kahan proposes an explicit deal between gun-control and gun-rights proponents: "In exchange for control proponents acknowledging that the Second Amendment creates a genuine *individual* right to gun ownership, control opponents should assent to universal registration of hand guns." Or, even more modestly, gun-control proponents could support an individual right to gun ownership coupled with the prevalent "reasonableness" standard state courts apply to gun regulations.

These strategies have one important advantage, and several important disadvantages. The advantage arises from the fact that slippery-slope arguments play a large role in anti–gun-control rhetoric. Propose a ban on private ownership of assault weapons, for example, and gun-rights advocates will say that the theory under which the government can prohibit ownership of such weapons would also justify a ban on handgun ownership. This proposal, they say, is "the first step toward . . . a federal police force disarming the law-abiding public." A firm commitment to the proposition that the Second Amendment prohibits a national gun confiscation law would undermine the appeal of such slippery-slope arguments.

One disadvantage of the strategy I've suggested is that gun-rights proponents would certainly doubt the sincerity of the commitment, made by adversaries who have spent more than thirty years deriding the individual-rights interpretation of the Second Amendment. Gun-rights proponents could therefore continue to make slippery-slope arguments without embarrassment, simply adding a line or two about their adversaries' hypocrisy.

A more important disadvantage is that gun-control proponents might not be able to control the individual-rights theory once they sign on to it. *They* might think that their position doesn't imply that gun registration laws or local bans on gun ownership are unconstitutional, but how can they be sure that courts will agree? As Chapters 1 and 2 showed, the contours of the individual-rights view are ill-defined, largely because its proponents have devoted most of their effort to creating the Standard Model and not much to elaborating what that model implies about particular forms of gun control. Gun-control proponents who committed themselves to the individual-rights view would be buying a pig in a poke. Better, they might think, to continue to fight the good fight over the collective-rights view.

And finally, who could make and enforce deals like the one Kahan proposes? Why should gun-control proponents think that if *they* sign on to the individual-rights view, gun-rights proponents will accept universal registration? (And of course, if gun-rights proponents say they believe that reasonable regulations of gun ownership are consistent with the individual-rights view, why should they think that gun-control proponents will abandon the collective-rights view and give up on the prospect of complete confiscation?)

A third set of poll results suggests a different strategy.

• On scattered polls that ask the question, the public appears to be about evenly divided between people who think the government should enforce existing laws more effectively but not adopt any new regulations, and people who agree that existing laws should be enforced more effectively but also think that it would be good to adopt new gun-control laws, with a slightly larger number in the first group. And the public also appears to be equally divided over whether stricter gun laws would reduce the amount of violent crime, with a slightly large number thinking they would.

I interpret these polls to be consistent with the evidence we examined in Chapter 4 on the actual effects of gun policy on violence. We saw there that gun policies of any sort probably have relatively little effect on the level of gun violence, not to mention violent crime. The public, it seems, understands that not much is going to happen if our legislators and law enforcement officials focus on guns themselves. So they want more effective gun policies, but don't expect much to come of such policies.

This suggests a strategy of mutual disarmament, so to speak. The public believes, probably correctly, that nothing much is really at stake in fights over gun policy. We can be sure that a proposal to require that gun owners pass a licensing test would generate heated opposition and equally heated support, even though its likely effect on crime and violence would be trivial. And more generally, whether gun-rights advocates or gun-control advocates won lots of battles, the levels of crime and violence would be pretty much the same. So maybe we should simply turn our attention to other policies that might be more effective in fighting crime and violence: more police on the streets, ensuring that young people have better access to education and jobs, more disparagement by leading public figures of violence on television and in movies, or whatever else serious inquiry into the causes of crime and violence reveals to be somewhat effective policies. This is not a book about such policies, and I don't know whether there are any decent effective ones. But, it seems, gun policies aren't all that effective, and fighting over them might simply be a diversion from efforts that *might* be more effective.

Mutual disarmament is hard to police: Trust but verify, Ronald Reagan told us. Somewhere, sometime, there's going to be a politician—probably more than one—who thinks that his career would take off if he pushed for a ban on gun ownership or for a "concealed carry" law. Perhaps gun-rights and gun-control groups could make it clear that they don't support such efforts and that neither side would take it badly were the other to oppose the adoption of these proposals. That way no interest group would be pushing for the adoption of new laws, and the fact that some interest groups would oppose new proposals wouldn't reignite the culture wars battle over gun policy.

Unfortunately, once interest groups are in the picture, mutual disarmament might be impossible. Interest groups exist to do something, not to sit idly by. What would be left for the Brady Campaign (remember, formerly Handgun Control) to do if its leaders took the position that they weren't going to support the adoption of any new gun-control policies? How could the National Rifle Association continue its large operation if it couldn't raise money by saying that a full pot of funds was needed to stave off gun confiscation policies? Maybe the interest groups could morph into something new, as the March of Dimes did when it shifted from raising money to fight polio to raising money to fight birth defects after a polio vaccine was discovered. But, not surprisingly, we can't expect interest group leaders themselves to adopt stances that threaten to put them out of business.

Political scientist Morris Fiorina suggests a different take on the policy questions. He interprets polling results on gun control and many issues dealing with the entire range of issues ordinarily discussed as involving the culture wars to indicate that there may not be a culture war going on at all—or at least not a culture war that tracks conventional political divisions. As he writes, "A solid majority of blue state voters support stricter gun-control laws, but so does a narrow majority of red state voters." And, he shows, this sort of agreement exists not merely in states taken as units but among individual voters as well. Why, then, are policy discussions so heated? Because, Fiorina argues, interest groups have reasons to emphasize divisions rather than agreements.

The dynamics were clear immediately after the campus shootings at Virginia Tech University in April 2007. The *New York Times* editorialized in favor of "stronger controls over the lethal weapons that cause such wasteful carnage," although it was unclear what controls short of a complete ban and confiscation of existing weapons could prevent recurrences of such tragic and isolated events. Perhaps there is here a faint hint of the "enforce the laws we have" strategy, for it turned out that the killer violated national law when he bought the guns he used, a violation that was made possible by an imperfection in Virginia state law.

Gun-rights supporters trotted out the "more guns, less crime" theory in criticizing campuses as "gun-free zones." James Wilson, the dissenter from the National Academy of Sciences committee report, wrote, "In one Mississippi high school, an armed administrator apprehended a school shooter. In a Pennsylvania high school, an armed merchant prevented further deaths. Would an armed teacher have prevented some of the deaths at Virginia Tech? We cannot know, but it is not unlikely." A serious social scientist would not write that final clause: Would there *have been* an armed teacher at Virginia Tech? In the area of the shootings? Able to bring down the killer? We cannot know indeed.

Can we cut the interest groups out of the conversation? Ordinarily we'd rely on *political* leaders to do that. But, Fiorina points out, political leaders are more extreme that the general electorate. With the decay of patronage politics, "today's party activists and contributors are less likely to be motivated by material rewards than previously." Instead, they are pushed into activism by their policy commitments, which are reinforced by the support they get from the interest groups I've mentioned. Gerrymandering of election districts to produce "safe" seats matters as well. Candidates chosen in the primary election conducted for the dominant party in the district are essentially guaranteed election. The voters in party primaries are the most committed and are typically not centrists. Candidates in primary elections appeal to a "base" that is farther to the right or to the left than the district as a whole, and so are themselves more extreme than the district.

All this makes it unlikely that political leaders—at least those chosen in small districts—will support the policy-disarmament proposal. But "unlikely" doesn't mean "never." Perhaps a candidate for statewide or national office could say, "I'm neither for nor against gun control. Reducing crime and violence is important to me, but gun policy doesn't have anything to do with that. Elect me, and I'm going to vote against any new gun policies—against gun registration, against a concealed-carry law. Instead, I'm going to consult with the best thinkers about crime and violence, and follow their advice. Maybe we'll revive the '100,000 new cops' program that seemed to work well in the 1990s until we stopped funding it; maybe we'll come up with something else. But whatever we come up with, it's not going to be a policy about guns. That's simply off the table for me." Of course that candidate isn't going to raise any money from gun policy groups. But will those groups get any benefit from funding the candidate's opponent? Not if the polling results are reasonably accurate. The public seems to understand that gun policies don't matter much in their daily lives.

Leaders of the national Democratic Party, which is clearly more disadvantaged than the Republican Party when gun control issues are on the agenda, have seen their problem. After the Virginia Tech killings, Representative Rahm Emanuel, chair of the House Democratic caucus, said that "the top priority of his party's lawmakers is hiring more police to fight crime, not tougher gun control." Emanuel's difficulty, and that of any national Democratic leader, is to deal with important components in their party who think that gun control should have high priority. The Democratic Party's track record on gun-control issues will make it difficult to convince voters in the middle that the Party's new-found commitment to gun rights is sincere. And, of course, Republicans are happy to take advantage of Democrats' difficulties. Still, perhaps a national Republican figure might take a stand against the NRA—not against gun rights, but against the trivial policies pushed by the NRA each year—to direct the attention of voters in the middle to the candidate's sensible approach to important issues. For, as gun-rights Democrat Brian Schweitzer, the governor of Montana, put it after the Virginia Tech killings, it does no good for Republicans—or for the country—for their party to be seen as in the NRA's hip pocket.

Yet culture wars battles are not so much about what we ought to do as about who we are. As conservative Democrat Zell Miller put it in 2001, discussions of gun policy are "about *values* . . . about *who* you are and who you aren't." Here too interest groups and political leaders play an important, and not terribly attractive, role. They find it to their advantage to exaggerate the differences among us, trying to persuade some of us that we really are the kinds of people who need to build gun rights into our understanding of ourselves, and others that we really are the kinds of people who need to do the same with gun control.

The trick, as Kahan suggests, is to shift our conversation away from polarizing debates about what the Constitution means and what sorts of gun policies actually reduce violence, and toward a respectful acknowledgment of the disparate visions of the good society that pervade American society. In Kahan's words, we "must, in the spirit of genuine democratic deliberation, appeal to one another for understanding and seek policies that accommodate [our] respective worldviews." As I've suggested, there *are* such policies. You can think of yourself as a cowboy or a social worker and think that 100,000 new cops is a good idea—the cowboy will imagine that the cops will be pulling their guns a lot, the social worker that they will be talking a lot. And the cops themselves will do what seems to work on the ground.

The difficulty lies in getting us to a place where *those* policies are at the center of our political discussions, instead of the policies and the constitutional arguments that interest groups and politicians use to mobilize their supporters. The poll results I have described indicate that we are not as polarized as some political leaders want to make us think we are. Perhaps someday soon a politician will think that saying exactly that is the way to win office. Or perhaps such a politician will think it advantageous not to make such a broad claim but to tell us that we needn't fight over gun policy, and that if we want to continue to fight the culture wars, there are plenty of other battlegrounds. Maybe once we come to think both that *something* needs to be done to reduce crime and violence, and that the proposals routinely placed on the policy agenda, including gun policies, simply aren't going to be adopted—or, if adopted, aren't going to do much—some politician will see the opportunity and grab it.

Notes

...

INTRODUCTION

Kerry photo op and Bush spokesman's comment: Described in Lois Romano, "Kerry Hunting Trip Sets Sights on Swing Voters," *Washington Post*, October 21, 2004.

"a matter of culture": George W. Bush in the second Gore-Bush presidential debate, October 11, 2000, available at http://www.debates.org/pages/trans2000b.html (visited September 5, 2006).

"Before writing this book": I follow here the practice described by Harry L. Wilson, *Guns, Gun Control, and Elections: The Politics and Policy of Firearms* (Lanham, MD: Rowman & Littlefield, 2007), at p. xi.

Lund: Nelson Lund, "The Past and Future of the Individual's Right to Bear Arms," 31 *University of Georgia Law Review* 1 (1996), at p. 20.

Van Alstyne: William Van Alstyne, "The Second Amendment and the Personal Right to Arms," 43 *Duke Law Journal* 1236 (1994), at p. 1236.

Insurrectionists: See, for example, Dennis A. Henigan, "Arms, Anarchy and the Second Amendment," 26 *Valparaiso Law Review* 107 (1991), at p. 110. Henigan was at the time the Director of the Legal Action Project at the Center to Prevent Handgun Violence.

"Of Holocausts" article: Daniel D. Polsby and Don B. Kates, Jr., "Of Holocausts and Gun Control," 75 *Washington University Law Quarterly* 1237 (1997). Polsby is now dean of the George Mason University Law School; Kates is a prominent litigator in gun-rights cases and has published a large number of important articles defending the gun-rights position.

Gun-control fascists: Searching Google for the phrase "gun control fascists" turns up a number of relevant sites, such as http://www. a-human-right.com/guncontrol.html (visited May 1, 2006).

Distinguished federal judge: Alex Kozinski, dissenting from the denial of rehearing en banc in *Silveira v. Lockyer*, 328 F.3d 567, 569–70 (9th Cir. 2003).

Treason argument: See, for example, Garry Wills, "To Keep and Bear Arms," *New York Review of Books*, 42, no. 14 (September 21, 1995), at p. 70 ("Tyrannicides do not take their warrant from the tyrant's writ....[T]he pre-government right of resistance replaces governmental regulation *including the Second Amendment.*"); Henigan, "Arms, Anarchy," at p. 128 ("the existence of a constitutional right to use arms against tyranny would, itself, create the conditions for tyranny").

CHAPTER 1

OLC Memorandum: "Whether the Second Amendment Secures an Individual Right," August 24, 2004, available at www.usdoj.gov/olc/ secondamendment2.htm.

Fourth Amendment decision: *United States v. Verdugo-Urquidez*, 494 U.S. 259 (1990).

Right to breed and keep horses: The example is drawn from H. Richard Uviller and William G. Merkel, *The Militia and the Right to Arms, or, How the Second Amendment Fell Silent* (Durham, NC: Duke University Press, 2002). Uviller and Merkel treat the Second Amendment's preamble as a condition, not an explanation.

New Hampshire Constitution: Quoted, along with many similar preambulatory phrases, in Eugene Volokh, "The Commonplace Second Amendment," 73 *New York University Law Review* 793 (1998).

Lockean theory: The theory of checks and balances plays into the interpretation of the Second Amendment offered by gun-control proponents, as we'll see in Chapter 2. In addition, the new Constitution conceited judicial review from a minor into a fundamental institution in a free society. The idea of judicial review isn't an important part of the Second Amendment story, and so I won't deal with it in any additional detail. Chapter 2 explains why even the practice of judicial review isn't really a part of that story.

Blackstone: I quote from the standard version, available at http://www.yale.edu/lawweb/avalon/blackstone/bk1ch1.htm (visited June 20, 2006).

"omnium gatherum": Garry Wills, "To Keep and Bear Arms," *New York Review of Books*, 42, no. 14 (September 21, 1995), at p. 65.

"widely circulated": Saul Cornell, "Commonplace or Anachronism: The Standard Model, the Second Amendment, and the Problem of History in Contemporary Constitutional Theory," 16 *Constitutional Commentary* 221 (1999), at pp. 232–33.

Story: Para. 1890, available at http://www.constitution.org/js/js_344.htm (visited June 20, 2006). Story has a second paragraph on the Second Amendment, describing the British Bill of Rights' provision on bearing arms as "at present . . . more nominal than real."

Early state constitutional provisions: These are widely available, including at http://www.law.ucla.edu/volokh/beararms/statecon.htm (visited June 20, 2006).

District of Columbia decision: *Parker v. District of Columbia*, No. 04-7041 (D.C. Cir., March 9, 2007).

Natty Bumppo episode: *The Pioneers*, ch. 30. I have simplified the episode a bit.

CHAPTER 2

David Williams's argument: David Williams, *The Mythic Meanings of the Second Amendment: Taming Political Violence in a Constitutional Republic* (New Haven, CT: Yale University Press, 2003).

"meaningless" and "outdated": David C. Williams, "Civic Republicanism and the Citizen Militia: The Terrifying Second Amendment," 101 *Yale Law Journal* 551 (1991), at pp. 554–55.

"outlived its application": Uviller and Merkel, p. 154.

Banning armor-piercing bullets: Don B. Kates, Jr., "The Second Amendment: A Dialogue," 49 *Law and Contemporary Problems* 143 (Winter, 1986), at pp. 146–47.

Response: Stephen B. Halbrook, "What the Framers Intended: A Linguistic Analysis of the Right to 'Bear Arms,'" 49 *Law and Contemporary Problems* 151 (Winter, 1986), at pp. 159–60.

Citizen-related view: I rely on the arguments developed in Saul Cornell, *A Well-Regulated Militia: The Founding Fathers and the Origins of Gun Control in America* (New York: Oxford University Press, 2006).

Washington letter: Quoted in Uviller and Merkel, p. 59.

Barron: *Barron v. Mayor and City Council of Baltimore*, 32 U.S. (7 Pet.) 243 (1833).

Bushrod Washington decision: *Corfield v. Coryell*, 6 Fed. Cas. 546 (No. 3,230) (C.C.E.D. Pa., 1823). No one contends that the one-word difference between the original "privileges and immunities" clause and the Fourteenth Amendment's "privileges or immunities" clause has any substantive significance.

Role of juries: Akhil Amar, *The Bill of Rights: Creation and Reconstruction* (New Haven: Yale University Press, 1998), emphasizes the way in which the Second Amendment and the right to jury trial are complementary expressions of the Bill of Rights commitment to control by citizens over their government.

CHAPTER 3

In addition to the materials specifically cited below, the best summary presentation of the collective-rights interpretation of the Second Amendment is Michael C. Dorf, "What Does the Second Amendment Mean Today?," 76 *Chicago-Kent Law Review* 291 (2000).

Brady statement: Press release quoted in U.S. Newswire, July 11, 2001, available at http://w3.lexis.com/lawschoolreg/researchlogin04.asp (visited May 8, 2006).

"linguistic tricks": Garry Wills, "To Keep and Bear Arms," *New York Review of Books*, 42, no. 14 (September 21, 1995), at p. 72.

Shays's Rebellion: For details, see Leonard Richards, *Shays' Rebellion: The American Revolution's Final Battle* (Philadelphia: University of Pennsylvania Press, 2002).

Whiskey Rebellion: For details, see Thomas P. Slaughter, *The Whiskey Rebellion: Frontier Epilogue to the American Revolution* (New York: Oxford University Press, 1986).

National Guard argument: This is well developed in H. Richard Uviller and William G. Merkel, *The Militia and the Right to Arms, or, How the Second Amendment Fell Silent* (Durham, NC: Duke University Press, 2002).

Houston v. Moore: 18 U.S. (18 Wheat.) 1 (1820).

First gun-control movement: I rely on Saul Cornell, *A Well-Regulated Militia: The Founding Fathers and the Origins of Gun Control in America* (New York: Oxford University Press, 2006).

Tennessee Supreme Court decision: *Aymette v. Tennessee*, 21 Tenn. (2 Hum.) 154 (1840).

Arkansas Supreme Court decision: *State v. Buzzard*, 4 Ark. (2 Pike) 18 (1842).

Presser v. Illinois: 116 U.S. 252 (1886).

United States v. Miller: 307 U.S. 174 (1939).

Machine gun decision: *United States v. Rybar*, 103 F.3d 273 (3rd Cir. 1996). The Supreme Court denied review of Rybar's conviction, 522 U.S. 807 (1997).

Background on Morton Grove ordinance: Nathaniel Sheppard, Jr., "Illinois Town Faces Lawsuit after Limiting Pistol Use," *New York Times*, July 4, 1981, p. A-6.

Quilici v. Morton Grove: 695 F.2d 261 (7th Cir. 1982), cert. denied, 464 U.S. 863 (1983).

"Residents could go": Mayor Sigel Davis of Bellwood, Illinois, quoted in Sheppard, "Illinois Town."

Roberti-Roos Act challenge: *Silveira v. Lockyer*, 312 F.3d 1052 (9th Cir. 2002), rehearing en banc denied, 328 F.3d 567 (9th Cir. 2003), cert. denied, 540 U.S. 1046 (2003).

First Amendment and prior restraints: The classic treatment, confirmed by later scholarship, is Leonard Levy, *Legacy of Suppression: Freedom of Speech and Press in Early American History* (Cambridge, MA: Harvard University Press, 1960). Levy modified some of his conclusions, though not the one referred to here, in *Emergence of a Free Press* (New York: Oxford University Press, 1985).

"Faint-hearted" originalism: The phrase comes from Antonin Scalia, "Originalism: The Lesser Evil," 57 *University of Cincinnati Law Review* 849 (1989).

Breyer on constitutional interpretation: Stephen Breyer, *Active Liberty: Interpreting Our Democratic Constitution* (New York: Alfred Knopf, 2005), pp. 7–8.

1991 study: Glenn A. Phelps and John B. Gates, "The Myth of Jurisprudence: Interpretive Theory in the Constitutional Opinions of Justice Rehnquist and Brennan," 31 *Santa Clara Law Review* 567 (1991).

CHAPTER 4

In addition to the materials cited here, Harry L. Wilson, *Guns, Gun Control, and Elections: The Politics and Policy of Firearms* (Lanham, MD: Rowman & Littlefield, 2007), provides a good overview of additional gun-related policies and the politics associated with them.

Khalid Ali shooting: "Three Face Charges Surrounding Death of Teen," available at http://wgrz.com/news/news_article.aspx?storyid= 35449 (visited June 22, 2006).

Thomas Sampson shootings: Natasha Lee, "2 Are Shot to Death at Maintenance Yard," *Los Angeles Times*, February 22, 2005, p. B-1; Erica Williams, "Double Slaying Another Blow for City Workers," *Los Angeles Times*, February 26, 2005, p. B-3; "Man Expected to Be Charged with Murder in Slayings of City Employees," City News Service, February 28, 2005, available in LEXIS/NEXIS, "News, Most Recent Two Years" file.

Barron Whiteman shooting: Clea Benson, "Wounded Bartender Kills Robber When His Gun Jams," *Philadelphia Inquirer*, January 23, 1997, p. R-1.

"free-lunch syndrome": Franklin E. Zimring, "Continuity and Change in the American Gun Debate," in *Guns, Crime, and Punishment in America*, ed. Bernard E. Harcourt (New York: New York University Press, 2003), at p. 33.

"Stand your ground" laws: For a description, see Adam Liptak, "15 States Expand Right to Shoot in Self-Defense," *New York Times*, August 7, 2006, p. A-1.

Stigler quote: George J. Stigler, "The Conference Handbook," 85 *Journal of Political Economy* 441 (1977), at p. 442.

Crack and urban areas: The results are reported in Florenz Plassmann and John Whitley, "Confirming 'More Guns, Less Crime,'" 55 *Stanford Law Review* 1313 (2003), at pp. 1361–62.

Florida's impact on "must issue" results: Don A. Black and Daniel S. Nagin, "Do Right-to-Carry Laws Deter Violent Crime?," 27 *Journal of Legal Studies* 209 (1998), at p. 214.

Friedman on statistical significance: Quoted in Ian Ayres and John J. Donohue III, "Shooting Down the 'More Guns, Less Crime' Hypothesis," 55 *Stanford Law Review* 1191 (2003), at p. 1202, n. 16.

Statistical significance example: http://www.statpac.com/surveys/statistical-significance.htm (visited July 14, 2006).

2.5 million defensive gun uses: Gary Kleck and Marc Gertz, "Armed Resistance to Crime: The Prevalence and Nature of Self-Defense with a Gun," 86 *Journal of Criminal Law and Criminology* 150 (1993).

116,000 defensive gun uses: Reported in National Research Council (NRC) of the American Academies, *Firearms and Violence: A Critical Review* (Washington: National Academies Press, 2004), at p. 103.

Survey questions: Reported in NRC, *Firearms and Violence*, at pp. 103–5.

"95 percent confidence interval": Reported in NRC, *Firearms and Violence*, at pp. 112–13.

Explanation of confidence interval: Taken from Valerie J. Easton and John H. McCall, Statistics Glossary, vol.1, available at http://www.cas.lancs.ac.uk/glossary_v1.1/confint.html#confinterval (visited August 15, 2006).

Over-reporting defensive gun uses: David Hemenway, "Survey Research and Self-Defense Gun Use: An Explanation of Extreme Overestimates," 87 *Journal of Criminal Law and Criminology* 1430 (1997), at p. 1435.

"defender or perpetrator": NRC, *Firearms and Violence*, at p. 106.

Thirteen brandishers and thirty-eight victims: Philip J. Cook, Jens Ludwig, and Daniel Hemenway, "The Gun Debate's New Mythical Number: How Many Defensive Gun Uses Per Year?" 16 *Journal of Policy Analysis and Management* 463 (1997), at p. 467.

More than the total number of rapes: Cook, Ludwig, and Hemenway, "The Gun Debate's New Mythical Number," at p. 465.

"potentially troubling": NRC, *Firearms and Violence*, at p. 112.

"mythical number": Cook, Ludwig, and Hemenway, "The Gun Debate's New Mythical Number."

NRC committee's conclusions: NRC, *Firearms and Violence*, at pp. 2–3.

"More guns, less crime": The basic source is John R. Lott, Jr., *More Guns, Less Crime: Understanding Crime and Gun-Control Laws* (Chicago: University of Chicago Press, 1998). This work, issued in a second edition in 2002 with a response to critics, is based on an earlier study, John R. Lott, Jr., and David Mustard, "Crime, Deterrence, and Right-to-Carry Concealed Handguns," 26 *Journal of Law and Economics* 1 (1997).

"most cost effective method": Lott and Mustard, "Crime, Deterrence, and Right-to-Carry," at p. 65.

Dates of adoption of "must issue" laws: For a discussion of the coding issues, see Ayres and Donahue, "Shooting Down," at p. 1298.

"during the 1990s": Ayres and Donahue, "Shooting Down," at p. 1230.

Differences in later "must issue" laws: David M. Mustard, "Comment," Jens Ludwig and Philip J. Cook, eds., *Evaluating Gun Policy: Effects on Crime and Violence* (Washington: Brookings Institution Press, 2003), at pp. 328–29.

Statistical effects of including early adopters: Ayres and Donahue, "Shooting Down," at p. 1241.

"adopted by relatively low-crime states": Lott, *More Guns, Less Crime*, at p. 69.

"correlated with the presence of a shall-issue law": John J. Donahue III, "The Impact of Concealed-Carry Laws," in Ludwig and Cook, *Evaluating Gun Policy*, at p. 313.

"when the flawed instruments are dropped": Ayres and Donahue, "Shooting Down," at p. 1257.

"implausibly high": Donahue, "Impact of Concealed-Carry Laws," at p. 314. Here Donahue cites Dan A. Black and Daniel S. Nagin, "Do Right-to Carry Laws Deter Violent Crime?" as support for the claim of implausibility.

"special attention": NRC, *Firearms and Violence*, at p. 121. The material in the following five paragraphs comes from Chapter 6 of this report.

Broken Windows policing: For an account of the theory and its critics, see D.W. Miller, "Poking Holes in the Theory of 'Broken Windows,'" *Chronicle of Higher Education*, February 2001, available at http://chronicle.com/free/v47/i22/22a01401.htm (visited August 16, 2006).

"Lott's work convinces me": James Q. Wilson, "Guns and Bush," *Slate Politics*, October 13, 2000, available at http://slate.msn.com/?id=91132 (visited August 16, 2006).

"impose no costs and "not an econometrician"; James Q. Wilson, "Dissent," in NRC, *Firearms and Violence*, at pp. 270, 269.

"all of the studies": "Committee Response to Wilson's Dissent," in NRC, *Firearms and Violence*, at p. 274.

"typical gun permit holder": Donahue, "Impact of Concealed-Carry Laws," in Ludwig and Cook, eds., *Evaluating Gun Policy*, at p. 290.

"adoption of a right-to-carry law:" NRC, *Firearms and Violence*, at pp, 133, 134. The second quotation is "no effect" rather than "no discernible effect."

"almost unparalleled intensity": Daniel Polsby, quoted in James L. Meriner, "The Shootout," *Chicago Magazine*, August 2006, available at http://www.chicagomag.com/ME2/dirmod.asp?sid=&nm=&type=Pub Pagi&mod=Publications%3A%3AArticle+Title&mid=61BFC65300D24 DB58350C761094153A1&tier=4&id=47B61F0DF3B247D6AB98038FB5 DDEFFA (visited August 16, 2006).

Lott on NRC committee report: John R. Lott, Jr., "Shooting Blanks," *New York Post*, December 29, 2004.

Biased committee members: John R. Lott, Jr., *The Bias against Guns: Why Almost Everything You've Heard about Gun Control Is Wrong* (Washington, DC: Regnery, 2003), pp. 53–54.

"98 percent": John R. Lott, Jr., *More Guns, Less Crime* (Chicago: University of Chicago Press, 1998), p. 3.

Challenges to Lott's survey: I rely on the account provided by Jon Weiner, *Historians in Trouble: Plagiarism, Fraud, and Politics in the Ivory Tower* (New York: New Press, 2005).

Lott's lawsuit: David Glenn, "Scholarly Definitions Are Fighting Words in Gun-Law Theorist's Defamation Suit," *Chronicle of Higher Education*, April 20, 2006. This story describes Lott's departure from the American Enterprise Institute as "abrupt[]."

Flame wars: For a compilation, see http://scienceblogs.com/deltoid (search archives for "John Lott") (visited August 15, 2006).

"3,738 more rapes": John R. Lott, Jr., and John E Whitley, "Safe Storage Gun Laws: Accidental Deaths, Suicides, and Crime," 44 *Journal of Law and Economics* 659 (2001), at p. 678.

Reduction in accidental death: Peter Cummings et al., "State Gun Safe Storage Laws and Child Mortality due to Firearms," 278 (13) *Journal of the American Medical Association* 1084 (October 1, 1997).

NRC on safe-storage laws: NRC, *Firearms and Violence*, at pp. 218–19.

"NRA and ATF": John S. Baker, Jr., "State Police Powers and the Federalization of Local Crime," 72 *Temple Law Review* 673, 684 (1999).

Bush on Project Exile: Third presidential debate, available at http://www.presidency.ucsb.edu/showdebate.php?debateid=22 (visited June 22, 2006).

"Promising Strategies to Reduce Gun Violence": available at http://ojjdp.ncjrs.org/pubs/gun%5Fviolence/contents.html (visited June 22, 2006).

Republican Policy Committee: "Of Criminals and Guns: The 'Project Exile' Solution," September 30, 1998, available at http://www.senate.gov/~rpc/releases/1998/Exile-kf.htm (visited June 22, 2006).

Gun Owners of America: "Gun Owners Speak Out against Push for Project Exile Today," May 13, 2001, available at http://www.gunowners.org/pro109.htm (visited June 22, 2006). For other expressions of concern from gun-rights advocates, see "Alternatives to Gun Control: Enforcing the Laws We Already Have," available at http://www.guncite.com/gun_control_gcagenfo.html (visited June 22, 2006).

"feel-good, do-something": The phrase, taken from William Eskridge and Philip Frickey, is applied to gun policy by Sara Sun Beale, "The Unintended Consequences of Enhancing Gun Penalties: Shooting Down the Commerce Clause and Arming Federal Prosecutors, " 51 *Duke Law Journal* 1641 (March 2002), p. 1654.

Description of Project Exile and results: "Promising Strategies," profile no. 38; Daniel C. Richman, " 'Project Exile' and the Allocation of Federal Law Enforcement Authority," 43 *Arizona Law Review* 369 (2001), pp. 379–81.

Overfederalization: See, e.g., Beale, "Unintended Consequences"; Kathryn E. Jermann, "Project Exile and the Overfederalization of Crime," 10 *Kansas Journal of Law and Public Policy* 332 (2000).

"minor-grade police court": Senior District Judge Richard L. Williams, quoted in Richman, " 'Project Exile,' " p. 409, n. 272.

Petersburg, Virginia: *United States v. Jones*, 36 F. Supp. 2d 304, 316 (E.D. Va. 1999).

US News and World Report: Chitra Ragavan, "Ready, Aim, Misfire," *US News and World Report*, May 21, 2001, p. 16.

Study of Richmond murder rates. Steven Raphael and Jens Ludwig, "Prison Sentence Enhancements: The Case of Project Exile," in Ludwig and Cook, *Evaluating Gun Policy*, at p. 251.

"brings together police officers": "Promising Strategies," profile no. 48.

"saturation patrols:" "Promising Strategies," profile no. 28.

Police stops: "Promising Strategies," profile no. 23. For relevant Supreme Court precedents, see *Whren v. United States*, 517 U.S. 806 (1996), which found no constitutional violation in a "pretextual" stop of someone who had violated the traffic laws but who the police officers wanted to search for drugs; *City of Indianapolis v. Edmond*, 531 U.S. 32 (2000), which invalidated a system of neighborhood checkpoints at which all cars were stopped and examined for the presence of drugs.

Oakland gun dealers: "Promising Strategies," profile no. 16

Kansas City drive-by: "Promising Strategies," profile no. 20.

Indianapolis "adaptive behavior": "Promising Strategies," profile no. 23.

"let a thousand flowers bloom": Richman, " 'Project Exile,' " p, 383.

Boston program: "Promising Strategies," profiles no. 2 (which provides an overview of Boston's programs), 10, 21, 33, 46, and 58.

"We're here because of the shooting": Quoted in Richard Rosenfeld, Robert Fornango, and Eric Baumer, "Did Ceasefire, Compstat, and Exile Reduce Homicide?" 4 *Criminology & Public Policy* 419 (2005).

Evaluation of Operation Ceasefire and Project Exile: Rosenfeld et al., "Did Ceasefire, Compstat, and Exile Reduce Homicide?"

Levitt on causes of crime reduction: Steven D. Levitt and Stephen J. Dubner, *Freakonomics* (New York: Penguin, 2005), ch. 6.

Commercial test-preparation service: I used GunExams.com, available at http://www.gunexams.com (visited February 13, 2007).

"instantly fail the exam": http://www.guns.to/fac/exam.htm (visited February 28, 2007).

"Why does scientific evidence": Peter Greenwood, "Comment," in Ludwig and Cook, *Evaluating Gun Policy*, at p. 283.

Ayn Rand: For a collection of Rand's statements on gun policy, see http://www.noblesoul.com/orc/bio/biofaq.html#Q5.2.5 (visited June 29, 2006). The website's author summarizes Rand's position: "Rand never published a written statement about gun control, but her comments about it in response to questions suggest that she was skeptical of the idea but not strongly opposed to it."

Mountain climbing example: Dan M. Kahan and Donald Braman, "More Statistics, Less Persuasion: A Cultural Theory of Gun-Risk Perceptions," 151 *University of Pennsylvania Law Review* 1291 (2003), pp. 1295–96. Unless indicated, all additional quotations are from this article.

"Common values lead to common fears": Mary Douglas and Aaron Wildavsky, *Risk and Culture* (Berkeley: University of California Press, 1982), pp. 8–9.

Description of the three cultural views: These are drawn from Kahan and Braman, "More Statistics," p. 1297, and Aaron Wildavsky, "Choosing Preferences by Constructing Institutions: A Cultural Theory of Preference Formation," 81 *American Political Science Review* 1 (March, 1987).

Another study: Dan M. Kahan, Donald Braman, John Gastil, Paul Slovic, and C. K. Mertz, "Gender, Race, and Risk Perception: The Influence of Cultural Status Anxiety," Yale Law School, Public Law & Legal Theory Research Paper Series, Research Paper No. 86, available at http://ssrn.com/abstract=723721 (visited June 30, 2006).

"More statistics, less persuasion": Donald Braman and Dan M. Kahan, "Overcoming the Fear of Guns, the Fear of Gun Control, and the Fear of Cultural Politics: Constructing a Better Gun Debate," 55 *Emory Law Journal* 569 (2006), at p. 580.

Critics of cultural theory as applied to gun policy: Philip J. Cook and Jens Ludwig, "Fact-Free Gun Policy?," 151 *University of Pennsylvania Law Review* 1329 (2003). The quotations are from p. 1331.

Emerson case: *United States v. Emerson*, 270 F.3d 203 (5th Cir. 2001). The Supreme Court denied review of Dr. Emerson's appeal. 536 U.S. 907 (2002). The Department of Justice's response to his petition for review agreed that the Second Amendment protected an individual right, but urged denial of review until after a trial occurred. I draw some of the facts presented here from Uviller and Merkel, pp. 212–13.

Emerson's sentence: Described in "The Emerson Case," available at http://www.ejfi.org/emerson.htm (visited March 14, 2006).

New Orleans gun confiscations: For a collection of comments, see http://volokh.com/posts/chain_1126317466.shtml (visited September 3, 2006).

Federal statute on gun confiscations in emergencies: Homeland Security Appropriations Act 2007, sec. 557, codified at 42 U.S.C. § 5207.

State court interpretations of state constitutional rights to keep and bear arms: I rely on Adam Winkler, "Scrutinizing the Second Amendment," 105 *Michigan Law Review* 683 (2007).

Wisconsin case: *State v. Hamdan*, 2003 Wi. 113 (2003).

Gerry and "trained to arms": Quoted in Wills, "To Keep and Bear Arms," at p. 69.

CONCLUSION

Poll data: For summaries, see http://pollingreport.com/guns.htm and /guns2.htm (visited May 29, 2006).

Kahan proposal: Donald Braman and Dan M. Kahan, "Overcoming the Fear of Guns, the Fear of Gun Control, and the Fear of Cultural Politics: Constructing a Better Gun Debate," 55 *Emory Law Journal* 569 (2006), at p. 599.

"federal police force:" The statement is taken from an advertisement placed by the National Rifle Association in the magazine *American Rifleman*, in October 1993, and is quoted in Andrew D. Herz, "Gun Crazy: Constitutional False Consciousness and Dereliction of Dialogic Responsibility," 75 *Boston University Law Review* 57 (1995), at p. 86. Herz's position on gun control is indicated by his article's title.

Fiorina: Morris P. Fiorina, with Samuel J. Abrams and Jeremy C. Pope, *Culture War?: The Myth of a Polarized America* (New York: Pearson, Longman, 2005). The quotations are from pages 16 and 79.

"stronger controls": Editorial, "Eight Years After Columbine," *New York Times*, April 17, 2007, p. A-26.

"gun-free zones": David B. Kopel, " 'Gun-Free Zones,' " *Wall Street Journal*, April 18, 2007, p. A-17.

James Wilson: James Q. Wilson, "In Defense of Guns," *Los Angeles Times*, April 20, 2007, p. A-31.

"the top priority": Rahm Emanuel, *quoted in* Nicholas Johnston, "Emanuel Says Democrats to Focus on More Police, Not Gun Control," April 20, 2007, available at http://www.bloomberg.com/apps/news?pid=20601070&sid=aGquqgR_BDMc&refer=home (visited April 22, 2007).

Brian Schweitzer: Governor Schweitzer's comments were made on the Bill Maher show, HBO, April 20, 2007.

Zell Miller: Zell Miller, "The Democratic Party's Southern Problem," *New York Times*, June 4, 2001, p. A-17.

"spirit of genuine democratic deliberation": Dan M. Kahan and Donald Braman, "More Statistics, Less Persuasion: A Cultural Theory of Gun-Risk Perceptions," 151 *University of Pennsylvania Law Review* 1291, 1321 (2003).

Index

. . .